A Widow's Guide

Helping you choose the right path

Anita Gatehouse

Matador
9 Priory Business Park,
Wistow Road, Kibworth Beauchamp,
Leicestershire. LE8 0RX
Tel: (+44) 116 279 2299
Fax: (+44) 116 279 2277
Email: books@troubador.co.uk
Web: www.troubador.co.uk/matador

ISBN 978 1783060 030

British Library Cataloguing in Publication Data.
A catalogue record for this book is available from the British Library.

Typeset by Troubador Publishing Ltd, Leicester, UK

Matador is an imprint of Troubador Publishing Ltd

To Ron and Rita, I think you would be proud.

Praise for this book

"The personal finance world has long been waiting for a book that covers the money issues widows face in the wake of losing a loved one. This is the definitive book on the subject. Sensitively written and full of useful guidance."

Jeff Prestridge *Personal Finance Editor Mail on Sunday*

"With great care and empathy Anita delivers practical advice in a way that will enable even the most financially disorganised and in-experienced to quickly get to grips with their monetary affairs. And by breaking down what can seem like a herculean task into manageable chunks, she makes meaningful progress achievable and delivers it in the form of much needed "quick wins." A must have resource for anyone trying to sort out their finances after the death of a loved one."

Darren Baker *ACII APFS CFP   QED Wealth Management*

"When struck by grief, the confusion of dealing with paperwork, money and investments can be really overwhelming. Anita Gatehouse addresses the core issues and will take you through this process step by step. I wish I had this hugely valuable book when I lost my husband. It took me 3 months to sign vital investment documents because I was afraid of making a mistake. "A Widow's Guide" is beautifully written, navigating through the financial fog with ease. I plan to keep copies close at hand for all my bereavement clients."

Shelley J Whitehead - *Relationship / Bereavement Coach*

"Finally, a book that recognises the financial planning needs of widows. Though there are dozens of books for people keen on doing their own financial planning, they assume the reader is already knowledgeable, and they're interested. Widows are often neither, but still need to come to terms with budgeting, saving and investing. This book shows them how."

Dennis Hall *APFS AIFP MCSI Yellowtail Financial Planning*

Financial Planning is often made more difficult and frightening than it needs to be. There is too much jargon and "clever" ideas and not enough plain talking, understandable common sense planning. This is far from helpful and can result in people being too paralysed into avoiding facing their financial future. I am glad to say that Anita Gatehouse has managed to write a book which avoids all of these pitfalls and delivers exactly the information required in a clear and concise manner. The book manages to cover the important things that anyone recently widowed will need to know to get them through a very difficult time and set them on the road to a secure financial future. Anita focuses on taking positive action rather than talking about investment theory. The book is non-threatening and engaging for anyone who has little or no experience of finances and investment but there is enough meat on the bone that even seasoned investors will gain something. I would thoroughly recommend this book to anyone who needs to take control of their financial life.

Alan Dick *CFP(r) CERTIFIED FINANCIAL PLANNER*
Chartered Financial Planner
Forty Two Wealth Management
Vice President Institute of Financial Planning

Clarity and simplicity are watchwords used by Anita in her guide to what can be a bewildering subject at the best of times. Her forte is in breaking this down into manageable chunks which can be followed during a period of emotional distress. Usually, too much emphasis is placed on offering investment advice whilst having scant regard to your position now. Not Anita. She guides you through the essentials – those which need to be dealt with immediately and those to be dealt with when you feel ready to face the future. My wife, who was a widow when I met her, says how invaluable this book would have been had it been available when she most needed help.

James Martineau *FIFP, Certified Financial Planner*[CM]

Contents

Disclaimer and legal notice

This book does not intend to provide advice or recommendations but is general information on becoming financially organised. Everyone's circumstances are different and what is right for one person may not be suitable for another. Before taking any action you should seek the advice of a qualified financial planner, legal adviser or accountant. Tax rules and rates change and so will be different in time to those shown.

The author owns all rights in the text, designs, title and information included in this book. You may not copy, reproduce, modify, distribute, republish, display, post or transmit any part of this book without her permission.

The book contains details of websites, which are not under the control of and are not maintained by the author. The author does not make or offer any endorsement or give any warranties in respect of any products or services listed in this book and will not be liable for any loss whatsoever incurred by any person using such products or services.

Introduction

*A*s a financial planner, I've worked with many widows over the past 22 years and I've come to understand that irrespective of the robustness of their financial position, there are common difficulties and anxieties that all widows face.

Having to deal with grief at the same time as money, confusion over what's where, mountains of paperwork, lack of self-confidence, fear of facing poverty and how and where to start are just a few of the nightmares many widows face at this time. Perhaps surprisingly, many thought that they were the only ones to experience these fears and emotions.

So, I decided that if I was able to write about my own experiences with my widowed clients, helping them to become more financially well - organised and less fearful about handling money, it might be that this book could help more women move their lives forward with steadier, more speedy steps, bringing back a feeling of security. I do however appreciate that it is entirely different being a widow to knowing one, the pain is magnified a hundred fold and so I write with as much understanding as I can bring, having been supportive but not having fully experienced what you are going through.

Although this book concentrates on widows, of course anyone who has lost their partner whether they are male, female, married, in a civil partnership or not legally recognised as a spouse will face many of the same issues. So forgive the use of *widow* and *husband* in the book, I decided that by trying to cover every possible circumstance my message could be lost.

This book is not meant to teach you everything about money and investments, indeed most people, not just widows, benefit from the experience and wisdom of a suitable professional to guide them through the overload of today's information. But some straightforward knowledge, simple effective steps and understanding of mistakes to avoid will help you on your journey ahead. For some, parts of the book might be too basic but they are included as, for many, this information is needed and if you think, "Yes I know that" it might still be useful to have a different explanation.

The tax and legal aspects I have touched on, again, are to give you some basic information and understanding of things that may be totally unknown to you. Or, perhaps these things have never been explained well to you. Too many professionals fail to make sure that people understand and bamboozle and confuse them, so my simple drawings and analogies are there because I use them every day. They help me to explain things that I want people to understand. I actually use them with all of my clients; men, women, company directors, doctors, dentists, everyone because most people don't really understand money and it helps to see things pictorially. They do seem to work as people sometimes ask if they can keep the illustrations as looking at the picture brings back the understanding.

I believe the best way to get the most out of this book is to try and read through as many of the chapters as you can. Make a start on some of the ideas I recommend as you read through, going back to them as you are able to find the information that you will need, moving forward with the practical steps. I suggest that in time you re-read and redo some of the exercises, as you will be able to take on board more of the information and recognise that you really have been able to move ahead, feeling more in control of your financial future than you perhaps believe you will be now. Remember this is your book and although we have all been taught not to write in our printed books it's important for you to use this as a workbook, not just as a reading book, it will help to record and reconcile many things.

Don't be overwhelmed with how much is in this book, you will not be able to deal with everything straight away. It is a journey and for some, it will take longer than others and, you know what? That is okay. It's not a race, it's about building confidence and a firm foundation, the less anxious you are, the easier and quicker you will move through the healing process that you need to go through. If you can aim to learn enough to feel that you are not simply a passenger having to rely totally on family or friends, the difference it will make to your life, and theirs, will be dramatic.

In the book, I share with you examples of my own clients' stories, having changed their names to protect their privacy, which I hope you will find useful.

I sincerely hope that this book will serve as a navigation tool to help you emerge from the fog, looking ahead to a new and, by the nature of where you are now, a different life, at the same time creating an easier, more confident relationship with money.

Do the best you can and then move forward, go as far as you can see and then you will be able to see some more.

Anita

Foreword

A friend of mine, who had been widowed, kindly agreed to read through my draft book. The letter she sent me included some insights which I have, with her permission, included as a prologue, as I believe her words are very helpful and important.

"I am going to give you a few of my own experiences that I wish I had known, or someone had told me at the time.

Something that I think is important for the person to know is that they don't have to deal with everything straight away. Obviously their money management will need to be looked at as soon as possible, but other things can be put on one side for a while. Some people have their partner's clothes still in the wardrobe years later. It doesn't matter. Some things that are of sentimental value are kept, and their children will have to deal with these things when the second person dies. If you really don't want to get rid of something, you don't have to.

A very helpful letter I received from a friend of my husband, who had lost his wife, told me that when she had died, he felt as though the end of the world had come. But he went on to say that even though I would think it was rubbish, he knew that in time, I would feel better, and would be able to learn to live again.

I did not realise that I would feel physical pain, and when I told my doctor that I was really frightened that I was having a heart attack, she explained that that is why we call it broken-hearted.

I would advise anyone to accept help when it is offered. After a year of crying every day, I went to my doctor and said that I thought this wasn't normal. She told me that it was, and that most people cry in private, and put on a brave face around their family because they don't want to upset anyone else. In Victorian times the bereaved used to wear a black armband for some time so that people would know that they had lost someone, and so were more careful about what they said. Nowadays, no-one knows that you are dealing with a loss, and so sometimes something inappropriate is said, which is upsetting. Sometimes something insignificant to everyone else will happen, like a piece of music in the supermarket, and the person will abandon the trolley and walk away. I was offered counselling and found it helped me very much.

I would say to a new widow, that she shouldn't be too hard on herself. I beat myself up for not doing the right things, or saying the right things, and so on. My counsellor asked me to imagine my husband sitting in a chair near to us, and asked me 'What would he say about....' And of course I knew exactly what he would say about almost everything. She also asked me to imagine that I had died, and he was sitting with her and what would he have said, and again I knew and found a certain comfort from knowing that he would have felt about me, the same as I felt about him. It is a hard place to be when the very person that you would normally turn to when you have a problem, is the person who isn't there anymore, and isn't going to be ever again. Coming to terms with an important death takes time, and sometimes a bit of hard work.

Finally, I would encourage the person to try to arrange a social life for themselves. Not straight away, but when they feel ready. Join a group, a gardening club, a book club, or any other organisation that they may find an interest in. Try contacting old friends or colleagues whose company you enjoyed. Any interests that have been shelved for a while may be looked at again, and a new group of friends may result. The local newspaper will often have notices of exhibitions, and local activities, like drama groups, or a choir that may appeal to you.

Well Anita, I did find [your book] very helpful, and informative, and I wish you well with it.

With my best wishes,
J."

1

Shattered Emotions

"Death leaves a heartache no one can heal,
love leaves a memory no one can steal"

Irish saying

*D*uring the early days after the loss of your husband, you are likely to feel numb and completely overwhelmed. Words I have heard again and again are "lost", "paralysed", "disorientated", "angry", "weak", "guilty" and "disconnected". These words describe how widows like you feel or have felt and I truly believe that this is normal and, although it can be overwhelming, it's to be expected.

For women whose partners have always dealt with the family finances, these feelings will be significantly more intense, as facing the necessary financial "stuff" that makes up our lives without much knowledge and confidence can be absolutely terrifying.

Suddenly you're facing new responsibilities around money at a time when you're existing in a daze and it will all probably feel like a mountain too big to climb. If you've been used to dealing with your own financial affairs, take heart that you are already on steadier ground than many other women dealing with bereavement.

Fear about the future can be your biggest challenge and your greatest enemy as it can paralyse you from doing the things you need to do or propel you into making decisions too quickly, relying on friends and family for their advice.

You might find that you are alert and numb all at the same time, making necessary arrangements whilst functioning a bit like a robot.

Recognising some of the feelings that you are going through or that you have already experienced may be useful, knowing that these are normal human responses when you are hit with grief.

• There is a beginning, a middle and an end to grief and you have to go through it all to move beyond it.

- You will survive, though not without suffering.

- You will grow as a person, though not without the odd slip.

- You will make a life for yourself, though it won't be the same as before.

Try This

Look at the list of feelings and circle or underline those you have felt or are still feeling, it will help you to start piecing a picture together and when you re-read this book in the future, it may be that some of these feelings will have passed and will be a reminder that you have indeed moved ahead. We're all a bit guilty sometimes of not patting ourselves on the back for how far we've come and it's doubly important for you to do.

Disoriented – You feel confused, forgetting the simplest things like people's names or where you put your keys. You lose your bearings and think that you are going a bit mad.

Losing control – You feel like you are careering through space.

Disconnected – You feel like everyone else exists in a parallel universe to yours, you are on autopilot, simply going through the motions.

Overwhelmed – You have no idea where to begin, there seems so much that you have to think about and do. You are frightened in case you make the wrong decisions.

Angry – You're angry because your husband has left you and you are mad with him because he didn't show you where to find certain things and deal with life's "stuff".

Resentful – Other people still have their husbands, why don't you?

Anxious and fearful – What does the future look like? How will you cope? What about money? Will you have enough?

Guilty – You wish you could turn the clock back and do some things differently.

Numb and shocked – How can this have happened? Sometimes you expect to wake up and find none of this is really happening. You feel like you are living in some kind of bubble.

Denial – You just don't believe it. This can protect you for a while, helping you to not suffer too much reality too fast.

Physically sick – You are in physical pain and feel you can't eat as you feel so sick.

Vulnerable – You feel that you could easily be taken advantage of as you are so vulnerable.

Weak and exhausted – It takes all your willpower and energy to do the simplest things.

Overpowered – Everyone wants to give you advice and you find it's often conflicting.

Depressed – Waves of sadness come and go. Sometimes you can't even feed yourself or get dressed.

Lonely – Everything seems so empty, so many things remind you he is not here.

Acceptance – Some widows find themselves at this stage sooner than others, but eventually you will accept where you are and be ready to move on.

If you have been feeling weak and dog-tired, be willing to accept help and lean on people when you can. With a broken leg you lean on a crutch, with a broken heart you lean on family and friends. You may find that at times you simply want time alone to be able to grieve and feel the pain of your loss rather than being kept busy and in company, pushing the emotions away. If you feel you would like time alone, make sure that you arrange that with your family and friends, perhaps with someone ready to come over if you need them. A client of mine, Christine, had a signal when she wanted to be alone, she left her blinds down so that family and friends knew she preferred to be left by herself at that time.

If you have nursed your husband through illness, the loss of this role of care-giver can also add to your feeling of emptiness, no longer having that purpose in your own life.

It will be vitally important not to run away from your sadness, it will undoubtedly follow you, nipping at your heels, and might bite you later if you don't allow yourself to fully feel it now. In writing this book I realised that I had never really properly mourned the loss of my parents. When my mother died aged sixty, I had a very young baby and a two year old and I was the main breadwinner. I am also the eldest of four, the strong one who can cope and always knows what to do. I was fortunate to have my father around for seventeen more years, but once again I did not face my loss fully as it was too painful. And this was the grief of losing my parents not my husband as you have.

Well, I have cried a river researching and writing this book and I am relieved that I have been able to release my grief as I have no doubt that carrying it inside for such a long time was doing me no good. Looking back, it was lingering beneath the surface and burst forth occasionally but I didn't recognise what it was. It would have been better to have dealt with it at the time instead of putting on a brave face and appearing to be okay, organising and making sure everything was running smoothly.

If you feel that you are still disconnected with your life after some time try and find professional help. Your doctor may be able to recommend a bereavement counsellor who will be able to help you. I have included details of two counsellors in the resource section of the book, together with details of Cruse Bereavement Care, who also offer support to those who have lost someone.

By working through this book you can make sure you are not wasting your depleted energy. You can make sure you are focusing on the things that will bring your anxiety down and your confidence up and help you navigate through the financial fog, becoming responsible for your own financial decisions.

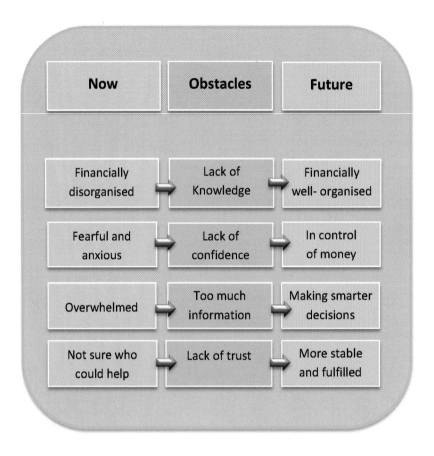

I want to get you from now to the future and show you how to make sure these obstacles don't stop you in your tracks.

"You can never cross the ocean unless you have the courage to lose sight of the shore"

Christopher Columbus

2

First Steps to Picking up the Pieces

"Start by doing what's necessary; then do what's possible;
and suddenly you are doing the impossible"

St Francis of Assisi

*A*s if you haven't enough to deal with, the realisation you are now responsible for looking after the finances may seem totally daunting. The natural tendency can sometimes be to try to find someone else to take on the responsibility for the finances rather than accepting that the role now rests in your own hands. You may feel resentful of the fact that you have now been placed in this position, particularly if you haven't had much to do with the household's finances.

While it can be helpful in the early stages of widowhood to delegate some responsibility to someone else, if possible try to remain involved, especially in the early stages, aiming in the long term to take control. It will be much more helpful to you in so many ways.

You will be glad you did at some point; you don't have to spend the rest of your life relying on others and in fact wouldn't actually want to if you thought you could be self-reliant. In my experience having control over your financial affairs leads to less anxiety and greater resilience in the future.

When thinking about your financial position you may find it helpful to separate it into your short-term needs (budgeting) and then your longer-term needs (future planning). Begin by concentrating on what is happening now and in the short term.

First steps to getting organised

One of the first simple steps to take during these early days is to buy, or ask someone to buy you a notebook that will fit in your bag. Make it bright so you can see it easily and begin to use this to note down information. Don't rely on your memory. This little notebook will become your beacon, use it to write down anything and everything that might help you, but don't use it to record PIN numbers unless you have a clever unbreakable code!

It can be easy to forget or not be able to find information that you need, for example, important names and telephone numbers. Use your book to make your life a little easier, keeping it with you to jot down things you are supposed to be doing. Take the time to use it and it will be a really helpful tool. Keep it to hand, for example, with your glasses or in your bag and make using it a habit.

Of course, you will find that people really want to help but they find it difficult to know what to do without guidance. With someone supporting you, use your book to write a list of things that need to be done and then try to delegate these tasks, writing down who is going to be asked to do what. Someone else can do this for you but if it is recorded, you can then look at the list if you need or want to.

If you have only very recently lost your husband, you are likely to be dealing with his estate, in other words all the items and assets that belonged to him. Depending on how you ran the financial side of your life together, this might be a completely unknown part of your marriage. Or it might be an area in which you were fully involved and engaged. The most difficult times are faced by those widows who have no or little understanding of the family's financial position, as they have to take on board more new information than the widow who, as sometimes is the case, was actually the money manager.

I haven't yet met one widow who, with help and guidance, did not, in time, become more confident and financially well organised and yes, *canny* with money. So take heart as we look at some of the steps you will need to take and for now let's assume that you are starting from scratch. If you are not, that's a bonus.

Begin with some straightforward organisation. For many widows they just don't know where to start. And remember, it doesn't have to be all be done in a day, face what you can when you can. Try not to sag under the weight of it all before you know how much there really is on your shoulders. There is a saying, "There's no one as poor as a new widow". It is so important to look properly at your financial position as only then will you know if your worries are realistic.

Once again, ask someone if you can't face doing this, but you need to buy yourself the tools to make your life easier, putting yourself in control. Buy a large lever-arch type two ring binder in a bright colour, an uplifting calendar and a two hole punch. You will also need some dividers that you will write on to make the information you're going to keep in your ring binder separated and easy to find. Buy some clear plastic wallets, the sort already punched with holes ready to file in your folder. You will also need two different coloured bright marker pens. One will be your "To do" colour and one will be your "Done" colour. Any book/stationery shop will sell all of these.

Like most people, you probably have folders and drawers full of paperwork that you and your husband built up over a lifetime.

As you sift through these, you will probably find that many of the papers are irrelevant or unnecessary. Most people never throw anything away in relation to their financial paperwork, they always think that they might need it. From now one of the most important things I want you to do, which will help you enormously, is to keep in your folder only the paperwork you are actually dealing with or that will be useful to you.

I can't stress how much this will help you to begin to feel in control. Lack of information and understanding intensifies fears and anxieties and contributes to remaining in a state of paralysis.

One day you may feel strong enough to grapple and tame the mountain of historical paper "stuff" you have. But right now by picking out only the papers you have to deal with and need at this moment, you will have a much smaller opponent to wrestle with and you will feel more organised because you will be, bit by bit, creating your own system that you know and understand.

Try to set up an area in your home that you can organise as a work area. Aim to keep it neat and tidy and don't be tempted to bring all the old "stuff" into this place. Be strict with yourself, remember just deal with the bits you have to, much of the old paperwork can wait.

How to start your own system

✓ Use a divider to make a section for your folder called "Current Account", hand write this on the divider tab.

✓ See if you can find the last 12 months' current account bank statements.

✓ For now, ignore the fact that there might be another 20 years' statements in the drawer or box. They will still be there if you need them or if you decide you don't, one day you will probably shred them.

✓ Put these twelve months' statements in date order in your folder, with the oldest statement at the back and the most recent one on the top.

✓ If there is more than one bank account, do the same for each one with a new divider labelled with a different name such as "My Account" or "Joint Account". If you can also find the cheque book and stubs that cover the last twelve months put these in one of the plastic wallets in the same section of your folder.

✓ This may seem to be rather simple but the truth is that is exactly how you need to keep it, simple and effective. You see, you might need to become a detective to work out what your husband's assets, pensions and life insurance and so on were and by having the last 12 months' current account bank statements you will be able to establish plenty of information to help you.

✓ Another useful document would be last year's tax return for both you and your husband if you normally have to fill one in. Again, create a section in your folder labelled "Tax Returns" and file last year's in there. Don't worry if you think you have not filled one in, not everyone needs to complete one. I just want you to have it to hand if there is one.

✓ If you come across your national insurance number or your husband's, write these straight into your notebook. You will need these so record them as soon as you see them shown on payslips or tax information, for example.

✓ Create a section in your folder for unpaid bills and another section for paid bills. Move the bills from the unpaid to the paid section as soon as you have done so, writing on them the date that they were paid.

You might be working with a solicitor or a member of your family might be dealing with your husband's estate. Normally, working with a solicitor will mean the process of sorting out the estate is likely to be easier as they will guide you through the process. It is often a good idea to ask a member of your family or a trusted friend to go with you to any solicitor meetings, as many widows feel quite disconnected with the procedures they have to be involved with around this time.

Remember to take your notebook and perhaps ask the person going to the meeting with you to make some notes in the book, especially listing the information or documents that your solicitor will need you to locate.

It will be important for you to find your voice and ask if you are not clear on something. These professionals will have helped many women like you and they will understand if you need some of the unfamiliar terminology and processes to be explained in more detail or for them to run through some points again. If you don't ask they will probably think you understand, so whatever you do make sure you are clear on the information. Do not feel embarrassed to check that you have understood.

You are the client, you are paying them to provide you with a service and they will want to serve you well. Remember they are dealing with this sort of thing every day; the chances are this is the first time you have had to do this.

If your husband left a will, this will show who he wanted to act as his executor or executors. This is the person or people he chose to deal with the organisation of everything he owns and they will carry out the wishes he recorded in his will. Once the initial paperwork is finished his executors will be given a legal document called a **Grant of Probate** which will then mean everything can be settled and paid out to whoever is to benefit after any bills are paid.

If your husband died without a will, there is a set of legal rules that will need to be followed, laying out how his estate will be paid out. These are called the **intestacy** rules. An application will need to be made to the court to grant **letters of administration** for the estate, which means that the court appoints a person, usually a close relative, as the "administrator" of the estate, who will carry out the same role as the executor under a will, but in this case there is a set "pecking order" for who will inherit.

When your husband's estate has finished going through the process of being settled, you may need to make some decisions about whether to keep certain investments or you might be asked questions about options relating to any pensions he had. This might be a good time to think about using a financial planner as once you make these sorts of decisions you might not be able to undo them.

Try not to rush into anything like this with a knee jerk reaction or rely too heavily on advice from other people. Their advice will be based on their experience, their own fears, their motivations – it will probably have little to do with the reality of your life even though it will be well-meaning.

I've included some guidance on how to find a suitable trusted adviser that you might find helpful in Chapter 11.

An early word of warning here. When any largish sum of money lands in your account, your bank will immediately be on the telephone. Listen politely to what they have to say on the phone but don't feel obliged to take any action quickly. Perhaps just ask the bank to "park" the money in an

instant access deposit account until you feel ready to make some decisions–
be prepared take note of Chapter 4.

After her husband died and money started to be paid into the bank account
from his employer's life insurance, one of my clients perceptively told me,
"I asked the bank employee who rang me, where had the service been for
the last twenty five years? Never a phone call in all that time!"

**As you begin to see what money there is, for almost all widows at this
stage, the biggest fear, no matter how wealthy they are, is, "Will I have
enough?"**

This is a big question, and one that you probably will not be able to answer
immediately. In fact, where do you begin to try? Many of my clients have
found that thinking about their money using a visual representation helps,
so I will describe this next and show you an example of what it might look
like. A little further on is a blank version of the picture for you to add your
own details. Go with me on this, it does help.

Visualising your money

I would like you to think about your finances like a water tank, it has pipes
with income flowing in and a tap through which your expenses flow out.

- Assets and investments make up the level sitting inside the tank.

- Any debts or loans you have will reduce the level in your tank. For now
  think of your home sitting *outside* your tank, because unless you, for
  example, sell and downsize, it won't add to the level sitting *in* the tank.
  You can't eat bricks!

- As you go through the process of dealing with your husband's estate, this
  will help you to work out what assets are to be passed across to you to sit
  inside your tank as a resource for your future alongside any of your own
  investments or deposit accounts, which will already be sitting in your tank.

The next step is to for you to find the details to build a clear picture of what's in your tank and how it's running, only then will you know if your money worries are realistic.

Try to focus your energy on getting this important picture sorted as it will form the basic foundation from which all other financial decisions will be made.

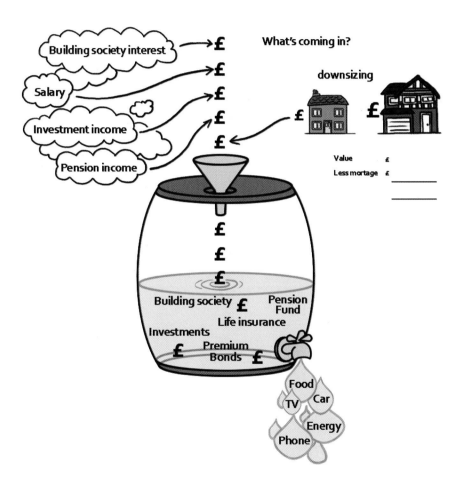

Working out your money flow

Start with your own **"Money Flow"** – what's coming in and what's going out.

Now those twelve months of bank statements and the chequebook stubs in your folder will be your best tools for the next step. If your husband was receiving a private pension, as part of sorting out his estate you will need to find out what happens to it now. Does it stop? Do you receive a reduced pension? You will need the answer to this to put the correct amount into the list below. If your husband was still working, again as part of the process of pulling together the information for his estate you will need to find out what widow's payments, if any, are going to be paid to you. You will be finding different pieces to the whole jigsaw of your financial position at different points in time and by having your own system, your folder, this book and your notebook you will begin to join the dots by recording the information as it comes to light.

You might be entitled to some government bereavement benefits. There is a comprehensive guide available on the Internet (details in the resources section of this book) or the Jobcentre Plus office will be able to give you a copy.

What's coming in?

Use this list to put together a picture of what's coming in based on what you currently know and add to it as you find out more information.

Of course, not all these items will apply to you but it will serve as a reminder of what you need to look for. I recommend you cross through any items that you know definitely don't apply to you to make it easier to see your own picture.

Try to put all your figures into monthly amounts as this will help create your budget plan.

MONEY COMING IN		
Your Salary (take home after tax)	£	per month
State Pension	£	per month
Other State Benefits	£	per month
Private Pension after tax	£	per month
Investment Income	£	per month
Other Income	£	per month
Total income	£	**per month**

It will be useful for you to have some basic knowledge about how your income tax is worked out, as some of the ideas on making your money work harder make more sense if you have an idea of how and where you pay income tax. I will cover this in Chapter 6. By using the information you have put together above you are well on the way to having what you need to be able to see where you fit in the income tax ladder.

What's going out?

Again, use the bank statements and cheque book stubs to build a picture of your expenses. I have broken most of your likely expenses into two groups for now:

- basic needs

- personal/leisure costs

Some of the expenses listed in the next worksheet in this chapter may not apply to you but work through the list so that you can try to cover everything. Again cross out the ones you definitely know don't apply to you. You may well have expenses that are not on the list, add these to the bottom so they are not overlooked.

Some of these expenses will be paid every quarter or just once a year, when you have found out what the cost has been for the last year using the bank statements and cheque book stubs, use that total and divide by twelve to give you an average amount for a month.

When you look at this list of outgoings, mark the ones that need to be changed into your own name in your "To do" colour. And make sure that if they are paid by direct debit automatically from an account just in your husband's name, you make contact with the supplier to change them to an account in your name.

There may be subscriptions that you need to cancel if they are in your husband's name and they are not something that apply to you. You would be wise to send them a letter as well as arranging to cancel the payment with the bank. This is so that their "unpaid subscription department" doesn't issue an automated letter writing to ask if your husband has changed banks or something, as receiving post for him can be upsetting. Unfortunately, you will find that there are many crazy rules that will drive you mad as you try to explain your situation. Common sense doesn't seem to exist anymore so writing a letter is often the least stressful road to sorting some things out.

Keeping records: In-comings and out-goings

A computer is a useful tool for storing records of letters you send out but don't worry if you are not computer savvy (yet), as there are other things you can do. It might make sense to buy an inexpensive copier/ printer so you can keep copies of the correspondence you send, filing the copies in the appropriate section of your folder. The cost of this type of equipment has gone right down over the last few years and any teenager in your family or a friends' family will have all the know-how to set it up for you and show you how it works.

Use your calendar to record dates on which you did things, as it can sometimes be really useful to know and you are unlikely to remember. Put another note in the calendar if you are expecting to have received something back, to remind you that you are expecting a reply. You will need to try and remember to check the calendar every couple of days. If you get to grips with using it, this will be a big help in being able to feel a bit more relaxed in terms of knowing what is going on without having to try and keep things in your head.

Use this list below as a reminder of which things you have sorted out as well; tick them as these are moved into your name in your "Done" colour so you feel you know where you are with the changes that will need to happen. But don't tick them off until you see something that confirms that the change has been made, this way you might spot when you think it should have happened and it hasn't.

BASIC NEEDS

Divide anything you pay quarterly by three to give you the monthly equivalent. Anything you pay annually, divide by twelve.

Mortgage/Rent	£	per month
Other loans	£	per month
Council tax	£	per month
Electricity average	£	per month
Gas average	£	per month
Oil average	£	per month
Water rates	£	per month
Food	£	per month
House contents/buildings insurance	£	per month
Telephone	£	per month
Mobile phone	£	per month
TV license	£	per month
Car Insurance	£	per month
Car fuel	£	per month
Car tax	£	per month

Car service	£	per month
Car finance	£	per month
Car recovery eg AA	£	per month
Children's costs/ child care/school fees	£	per month
Children's clothes	£	per month
....	£	per month
....	£	per month
....	£	per month
TOTAL	£	per month

PERSONAL EXPENSES AND LEISURE COSTS

Hairdresser	£	per month
Clothes	£	per month
Sports and hobbies	£	per month
Internet	£	per month
Satellite TV	£	per month
Holidays	£	per month

Subscriptions	£	per month
....	£	per month
....	£	per month
....	£	per month
....	£	per month
TOTAL	£	per month

TOTAL MONTHLY SUMMARY

What's coming in?	£	per month
What's going out?	£	per month

Now also think about each year, so multiply your monthly totals by 12 to give you annual figures to put in the spaces below.

TOTAL ANNUAL SUMMARY

What's coming in?	£	per year
What's going out?	£	per year

This is a good start to having an idea of what comes in and out of your tank. It's also a good plan to ask a trusted member of your family or friend to help you check this through. Ideally, if you have decided to use a financial planner they would be able to check this for you and help you establish your income tax position too so that you know you are putting down an accurate figure for your income after tax.

List your assets and liabilities

Now we need to look at what is sitting in your tank, including those assets that you are going to receive from your husband's estate. You also need to factor in anything that you owe, for example a mortgage or a loan. Add to your list below any life insurance policy payment or lump of capital you are going to receive from your husband's pension.

As you find the paperwork for each asset as you sort out your husband's estate and establish what you have in your name, make a new section for each one in your folder. Only put in the folder the bare minimum so that it remains manageable, for now all you need is perhaps the latest statement of an investment or even just a sheet with the details written on there so that you have a record of what it is and which organisation holds it with any reference number.

ASSETS – WHAT YOU OWN	
Personal assets	£
House value	
Other property	
Cars	
Business assets	

CASH AND DEPOSITS	£
Bank account	
Building society accounts	
ISA accounts	
Premium bonds	
Expected life insurance	
Expected capital from pension	
INVESTMENTS	
Shares	
Unit trusts/OEICS	
Investment Bonds	
Stock market ISAs	
National Savings Certificates	

LIABILITIES – WHAT YOU OWE	
Mortgage on your home	
Mortgage on other property	
Credit card balances	
Hire purchase agreements	
Other loan balances	

If you do have loans and credit cards, fill in the table below so that you can see easily which ones are costing you the most money in interest payments. This will be vital information to help you identify which you should aim to pay off first or change to a lower interest or, ideally, 0% account.

Name of the card/loan	Outstanding balance	Interest rate	Minimum payment

Now you need to bring your figures together in the summary below:

Total of the assets you own	£
Subtract the total of the liabilities you owe	£
Makes your net worth	£

Fill in your 'Money Flow' picture

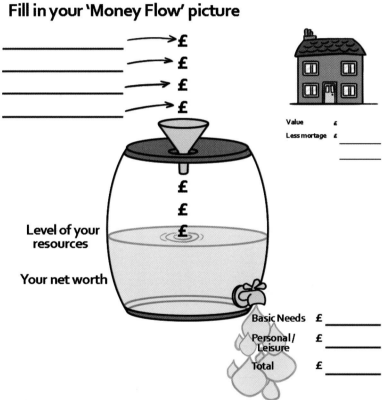

What to do now

- Is this the picture you expected?

- Is it telling you that you need to do something and do it fast?

- Do you need to get in touch with the benefits agency? If so, you will need someone to help you as it can be a difficult, laborious process.

- Does it look like it all works at the moment, spending about what you have coming in?

- Or does it say – Relax, money isn't your problem.

Looking at your own financial situation are you in a position to be able to take twelve months before having to make any major decisions? If so I urge you to take your time, you are much more likely to make sound decisions if you are able to make them further along your period of adjustment.

If you are not in a position to take your time and you need to take action because your financial position is not stable enough to wait, make sure you discuss what options you have with someone knowledgeable and trustworthy. Any decisions you make need to be made based on the facts about your position and you need to be exploring as many options as possible. Consider paying for expert independent financial advice, (see Chapter 10) which will help you decide on the right route and bring greater clarity to your position.

If debt is a significant problem, the Citizens Advice Bureau (CAB) can be very helpful. Another organisation, the Consumer Credit Counselling Service, which is a charity, also provides debt counselling and management services totally free. Their free Helpline number is 0800 138 1111.

Again, I recommend that you take a trusted friend or family member to any meetings like this, where they can make notes and discuss the options with you afterwards.

Do check whether you are in fact liable for your husband's debts before you pay them, discuss this with the CAB, the Consumer Credit Counselling Service or a lawyer.

This is not the time to be embarrassed about where you find yourself, this is the time to find some inner strength to accept it is where you are. By deciding to find out what you are able to do about it, you are less likely to end up with fewer options. The ostrich position is a much more vulnerable one than facing the facts.

Now that you have put together your net worth statement, this exercise should be carried out each year so that you can see if your net worth is growing or if you are losing ground. Once again by knowing your true position you will be able to make much, much better decisions.

"When faced with a challenge, look for a way, not a way out."

David Weatherford

3

Practical Money-saving Tips

"The world is round and the place which may seem like the end may also be only the beginning"

Ivy Baker Priest

*H*aving carried out your "Money Flow" exercise, you may be feeling that things are not quite as bad as you feared they would be, or alternatively it all may look worse than you thought.

No matter how your own picture looks, you are now in a position of having a clearer view and as anxiety often comes from fear of the unknown, this knowledge will put you into a place from which you can see things more clearly. Therefore you are already well on the way to being more financially well organised.

Whenever most people list out their income and outgoings (not many do!) they are almost always surprised at how much money seems to leak away unaccounted for, so if that is one of the thoughts that has come to you doing this exercise, you are not on your own. As you take control of your own finances there will be a strange satisfaction in plugging the leaks but it must be a positive effort, don't become a slave to it.

Practical ideas – "Every little helps!"

Below are some practical tips and ideas that could be useful. Some may be right for you to look at now, some you might want to circle in your "To do" colour to remind yourself to put them into action, if not now perhaps later, and then mark them off in your "Done" colour. You will find that you can only do these sorts of housekeeping jobs every now and again as the list is too long to be able to tackle them all at once, but over time as you look back through your book, you will be able to pick them up and do them.

Start to think in terms of mastering money and not letting money master *you* and you will begin to feel more in control little by little, making the most of your resources.

Having access to the Internet will be really useful and if you don't have that yet then ask someone if you can enlist their help to look up some of the information I suggest on lots of different topics. I have suggested some key websites in the list below, which are current as I write now in 2013, but which may change over time.

- If you are living by yourself and do not use significant amounts of water, having a water meter fitted might save you money. Check with your water supplier.

- If you are on a low income of less than £145.40 per week (2013) and you have reached state pension age, you may be able to claim Pension Credit to increase the amount you have to live on.

- You could qualify for more Pension Credit if, for example, you have a disability or own your own home and still have a mortgage to pay. You can check how much Pension Credit you might be eligible for by using the government's Pension Credit calculator.
www.direct.gov.uk/en/Pensionsandretirementplanning/PensionCredit/DG_180167

- If you can claim Pension Credit, you are likely also to qualify for some other benefits such as Council Tax Benefit and Housing Benefit. You can check the full range of benefits that you might be able to claim by using the government's online Benefits Adviser tool.
www.direct.gov.uk/en/diol1/doitonline/doitonlinebycategory/dg_172666w

- Keep the number of different bank and building society accounts you have to the minimum. You will feel more in control and be able to check that these accounts are working well with less effort on your part. Beware banks trying to encourage you to open a new account; they have targets to achieve! Ask them to put their recommendations in writing. This will buy you time to consider them and have a good look at what else is available before you fill in any forms. Check in the weekend papers for a top ten list of the best deposit accounts or use www.moneysaving expert.com. Remember that currently (2013) only up to £85,000 is covered if a bank fails and several banks come under the same license, which means you need to add them all up. Check with your bank to see which other banks are lumped together with them if you are not sure.

- Car insurance – check or ask someone to check for you on the Internet to see if you can get a better quote when your insurance comes up for renewal.

- House and contents insurance – check what cover you have and under what circumstances the policy/policies would pay out. Check a website like www.moneysupermarket.com to see if you can save any money when it is due for renewal.

- Utility bills, gas and electricity tariffs (charges) vary so check on the Internet whether you could change supplier and save. www.energywatch.org.uk and www.switchwithwhich.com

- Mobile phone contracts vary and when yours comes up for renewal check that based on your usage you have the most suitable contract.

- Think about reducing the amount of electricity you use by turning your appliances off rather than leaving them on standby.

- Credit card debt can be expensive as the interest rates charged are often high, your table of loans and credit card details will help you to see how much you owe and what interest rate you are being charged. If you are unable to pay off the balance see if it is possible to change to another card with a rate of 0% for a period of time. Try then to chip away as much as you can on the balance that you owe. Be careful to check the terms of the new card before you move your balance. www.moneysavingexpert.com have useful comparisons of different credit cards. Try to keep the number of cards you have to a minimum.

- New purchases – when you need to buy, say, a new fridge or kettle check on the Internet to find the cheapest version of what you want to buy. Try www.kelkoo.co.uk

- Make sure your home is well insulated. Grants are sometimes available. Check on www.government-grants.co.uk

- Petrol – find the cheapest petrol prices by signing up on the Internet with www.petrolprices.com

- Food - look at the Internet site www.lovefoodhatewaste.com for ideas on how to be smart and canny with food. This will be especially helpful adjusting to cooking for just yourself.

- If you can manage to find the energy to cook food from scratch make sure you make the most of your effort by freezing meal size portions for the times when you just can't be bothered.

- When it comes to Christmas and birthday presents suggest to your family that they buy you a National Trust or English Heritage membership, that will give you "free" places to visit all through the year and will keep you informed of interesting events.

- Decide who to go shopping with. This might sound strange but sometimes other people might encourage you to spend unnecessarily in an effort to make you, and them, feel better.

- Remember shopping is not the route to happiness. The term retail therapy is not correct; it is more likely to be a quick fix.

- Try to take only cash with you if you find it difficult to control your spending.

You may find that other people have tips that have helped them save money. Write them at the end of the list above so that when you feel you can start to turn this into a "To do" list you have more good ideas to try.

You may not be able to change the amount of money you have or the amount of income you have coming in, but you will be able to make sure your tank does not "leak". By tightening up the joints and using some of the suggestions above, you will be able to make some adjustments and make your money go further.

4

How to Avoid Costly Mistakes

"Even if you are on the right track,
you'll get run over if you just sit there!"

Will Rogers

*I*f you have been doing the exercises in this book, you will soon be in a position where you have the important information you need organised and filed away in your folder and have a clear picture of what's in your tank and what is going to be coming in and going out. You will feel a sense of achievement as you have already made real progress.

I've mentioned already that you need to be wary of making big financial decisions too quickly and I believe there are a few pointers that will help you avoid some common mistakes, to enable you to continue to work towards becoming more financially organised and in control, making good money decisions.

The first year is a period of adjustment and you are bound to make mistakes as you move through unknown territories but things will become more predictable and new patterns will emerge.

Costly mistakes in their different guises

- Check that your car insurance is still valid. If you were a named driver on your husband's policy you may not be covered.

- You may, as I mentioned before, have already been contacted by your bank when they see unusual amounts of money hitting your account, perhaps from life assurance policies or pensions. Be very wary at this stage – they may offer you tempting suggestions, and you may find yourself being talked into things. You must be able to recognise when the process you enter into is an investment *sales* process or an investment *advice* process. Imagine you're going to buy a car. You may go into a Ford dealership and discuss the various models they have on offer. The Ford salesmen is not going to tell you that based on what you need in a car, he thinks that a particular Volkswagen would be more suitable, that is not his job. He is there to try and sell you a Ford.

Most of the banks will work in the same way, and remember there is no such thing as free advice in this situation, irrespective of how anyone might try to convince you otherwise. Their earnings are often related to targets on bank products they sell. I have seen situations where the best advice for the client would have been to pay off some debts but that would not have been in the bank's best interests and an investment portfolio was arranged instead.

- Never give your credit card details or bank information to anyone who calls you, tell them you will contact the bank or credit card company yourself and then use the telephone number from your statement to tell them about the call.

- Never pay anything for a free prize, these are a con. Put the phone down.

- You may be surprised to know that one of your biggest enemies when thinking about your decisions around money is likely to be the news on television and the financial sections of the newspapers as they thrive on sensational bad news stories. The media can play a big part in your decision-making, sometimes without you realising that they have influenced the way you think about things. Remember they have lots of columns and minutes to fill and that generally bad news is more captivating to their audience than good. Focus on your personal economy not the global one.

  - Beware of experts sharing their top investment tips or making forecasts in the financial sections. These come with no "wealth warnings" and there is no link between wisdom and the size of the paper! Personal finance is more personal than it is finance; these gurus know nothing about your situation so take anything you read in these sections with a pinch of salt.

- Don't be a bank for others! Be careful not to make quick decisions on requests that may come from other people. Sometimes these might come from family members who perhaps think that you have more than you need. It is crucial that you take the time and the expert financial planning advice to establish whether you are in fact in a position to be able to do anything to help others. Make certain that you have enough resources for your own needs for the rest of your lifetime. It will always be wise to bring in a solicitor to help make sure that you are going about this type of action in a considered and formal manner if you do decide to help someone else financially.

- It might be useful to consider whether a deed of variation of your husband's will needs to be considered. This means that, assuming certain conditions are met, the original instructions in your late husband's will can be changed. There are times when organising a deed of variation of a will can be useful from an Inheritance tax planning or capital gains tax position and might be able to save significant amounts of tax. An example of this is if your husband has left money or assets to your children who are wealthy in their own right. They may prefer for your husband's gifts to skip their generation and go down to their children, your grandchildren instead, meaning that money passes down the family as tax efficiently as possible. This alteration to the way your late husband's estate is left has to be done within two years of his death. And again bring in a financial planner and solicitor to make sure everything is dealt with appropriately.

- Be wary of deciding to move house very quickly unless you are in a position where financially you have no choice, as buying the wrong house can be a very costly mistake. One of my clients, Pat, was desperate to move out of the home she had shared with her late husband but talking it through with me at length she realised she was trying to distance herself from her grief by thinking it would go away if she lived somewhere else. Once we got to the bottom of her motivation we were able to find the right support, enabling Pat to then take her time over the decision, instead of rushing headlong into buying a house without having time to think and adjust to what would be suitable for her to establish a different life. She was very grateful she did take her time as her choice of new home was very different after she gave herself time to grieve. There is no way to avoid some loneliness after bereavement but you might find that eventually living on your own doesn't automatically mean being lonely.

- Watch out for investments that seem too good to be true- that'll be because they are! If most accounts are paying between 1% and 3% interest a year and another offers 6%, the risks must be higher. The more vulnerable we are, the more likely we are to jump into something that seems to fit the bill and not ask questions. Logic can go out of the window because 6% seems so good.
  In this situation, you may not know the *right* questions to ask and that can put you at a real disadvantage.

✓ Ask how the yield (the amount of interest you will be paid) can be so high compared with other options.
✓ Are you committed for so many years?
✓ What happens if you need to get hold of your capital?
✓ Is there any possibility that you might lose any of your capital?

Remember, if the potential returns are higher, the potential risk is likely to be higher too.

- Don't get emotionally attached to your investments, use facts and not feelings to make decisions. For example, Amanda had very large outstanding mortgage with a high interest rate and no prospect of being able to move it elsewhere to try and lower the rate she was paying. She also had some money in a deposit account for emergencies and she had built up quite a sum in cash Individual Savings Accounts (ISAs), (I'll cover these later in another chapter). She was adamant that she wanted to keep her ISAs until we simply looked at the difference between the rate she was paying and the rate she was earning. She had not thought about comparing the two but once she saw the numbers she could see that the best thing for her to do was to pay off some of the mortgage and not be emotionally attached to her ISAs.

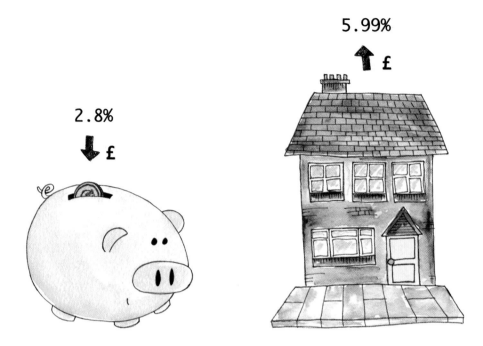

ISA interest earned vs Mortgage interest paid

Sometimes simple housekeeping is the best investment.

- Having done all that great work on creating your budget, make sure that you look at it again and try to keep good records of your costs in your filing system or in your note book so that you are able to update your figures each year. Do the same with your net worth statement too so that you know at what rate your tank is draining or, if it's going the other way and the level is rising. Remember that all your major financial and some of your life decisions are easier to make when you can see your up-to-date "Money Flow", so you need to make sure you keep it up to date.

Some widows come to me with all sorts of ideas and advice that well-meaning folk have given them and it can be easy when you are feeling vulnerable to be talked into doing things or get swept along with someone else's enthusiasm. Often only half the picture is shown; there are always disadvantages to any "good idea" and you need to know what these are. Keep in mind that it's really important before you make any decisions to give yourself time to find out and check with a professional if this "expert" guidance should be followed. Remember, one woman's meat is another woman's poison!

5

Your "Money Style" and Beliefs

"Don't feed your mind with negative thoughts.
If you do, you will come to believe them."

Catherine Pulsifer

*N*ow you have an outline picture of how your financial position looks and some mistakes to avoid, understanding how you think about money will be useful to help you look at areas where you are confident and areas where you may need to take extra care, or need help as you move forward looking after your own finances.

Some of your thoughts and beliefs around money are probably based on how money matters featured in your family growing up and then how money was dealt with during your life with your husband. For example, as a child and teenager, was money openly discussed within your family? Was it a source of arguments and anxiety? What about the years you and your husband were together? Open discussion? Difficult conversations?

Did you grow up thinking that women didn't really get involved with money matters? Or in contrast did your mother look after the finances?

Many of us have been brought up with the idea that talking about money is not polite, that it is a little vulgar. The reality is that feelings about money can run deep; they can be very complicated and confusing, and made more so if they cannot easily be discussed.

In certain religious groups, money is "the root of all evil" so if your upbringing was influenced in this way your own ideas around money may well be influenced. In fact, money can break up marriages, families, friendships and communities and yet you will hear people say "It's only money". It is often difficult to talk about a subject that we don't understand or that we think is likely to turn into a battle-ground and so it is often avoided or we talk past each other.

Depending on what era you grew up in will also have influenced the way you think about money. For example, those born before 1945 will have experienced times of scarcity and a make do and mend approach that was absolutely vital, as was being aware of the price of everything, never wanting to use credit.

Baby boomers born between around 1946 and 1965, on the other hand, want choice and are generally much happier than their parents with using credit or a mortgage to give them what they want.

Those born between 1965 and 1980 are known as "Generation X" and are generally more inclined to work to live rather than live to work, and money tends to be a means to an end not an end in itself.

So no two widows' philosophies around money will be the same, having been born at different times, had different upbringings and a different relationship with money within their marriage. Many women have been conditioned to be dependent, not independent, and it will be a new and uncomfortable role having to make financial decisions for themselves.

Without control over your money, and therefore your life, you are enslaved to those who understand it.

Some women who inherit substantial wealth from their husbands or life insurance payments sometimes struggle with the idea that it is blood money, feeling guilty that they have it instead of their husbands. This can create feelings of not being able to use the money, as they almost feel it's not theirs to spend. Some feel that they should be planning to pass as much as they can to their children when they themselves die. In my experience, most mature children would want their mothers to spend enough to live comfortably and find that it makes their own loss easier to come to terms with if Mum has what she needs.

So, if any thoughts like this are coming into your mind try to see that there will be a balance you can create given time.

The good news is that you are not sentenced to maintaining the beliefs

that you currently have, you may find that as you increase your knowledge and your confidence grows you will identify aspects that are actually a bit like the emperor's new clothes. You may realise that in fact he has been naked all along.

Try this

Jotting down some answers to the following questions might be helpful to work out where your thoughts around money have come from. Many of us grew up with sayings like, "Money doesn't grow on trees" or "You can't take it with you!" which may be influencing us more than we realise.

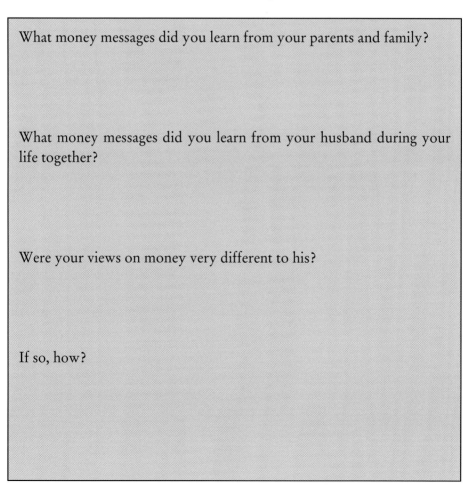

What money messages did you learn from your parents and family?

What money messages did you learn from your husband during your life together?

Were your views on money very different to his?

If so, how?

When were you most comfortable with money?

Why?

What has been the worst financial decision you have made?

Why?

What has been the best financial decision you have made?

Why?

Find your money personality type

According to experts in behavioural finance, we all fall into several different money *personality types*, a few of which I have described briefly below, along with helpful tips for each type. See if you think you recognise yourself in any of the descriptions, and bear in mind some of us fall into more than one type having had many influences in our lives.

HOARDERS

A hoarder is deeply attached to money, loves saving and seeing bank accounts grow. They often worry about outliving their money and may think that they never have enough to feel secure. They generally keep their money safe in the bank, not really thinking about inflation eating away at the real value of the capital. They find it hard to spend money on themselves and sometimes this extends to their family. Too much hoarding can lead to inner turmoil and bitter conflicts with family.

Helpful tips for a hoarder

- Look at your financial position properly; will you really run out of money? Study your Money Flow picture in Chapter 2 filled in with your own figures. Does it look okay? If you are not sure, think about finding an Independent Financial Planner (Chapter 10) to help you put your finances in perspective, so that you can stop fears about running out of money dominating your life.

- Spend time making sure you understand your big financial picture. Make sure your money has a chance of keeping up with inflation. If your financial position is actually more secure than you thought, try to relax and enjoy it without guilt or anxiety.

AVOIDERS

An avoider doesn't pay attention to money matters, ignoring financial issues rather than looking at them, leaving them alone, hoping that it will all work out. It is often the fear of what an avoider might find that stops them from taking the lid off their finances and looking inside. The thought of finding out they really do not have enough will dominate and depress so much that any kind of spending might become taboo and not enjoyable anymore. So, it's easiest not to look into the pot!

Some avoiders consider money to be evil and corruptive. Some think that having too much wealth or creating more wealth does not sit comfortably with their values, making them feel greedy and uncomfortable with the whole subject. Avoiders are not good at monitoring what they spend or how secure their future is likely to be and can alienate their families by not communicating about money. Some people just hate anything to do with numbers, often thinking that they don't understand them, quickly getting lost with them.

Helpful tips for an avoider

- It would be useful to think about what stops you from looking at this area of your life, as there may be many reasons. Do you feel inadequate making decisions, lacking knowledge you think you should have?

- If self-confidence is the problem, use the information in Chapter 10 to help you find the right financial planner, making sure that they can teach you to build your own capabilities with money.

- Do you feel that money is a distasteful issue, preferring to follow a more spiritual path? If your personal values are making money issues feel uncomfortable, then after you have made sure you have enough to keep you secure for your life, think about how much you could do to help causes close to your heart, making a real difference during your lifetime.

SPENDERS

Spenders often treat themselves in an effort to cheer up. Spenders don't always have the financial resources to use in the way that they do, building up debt over time, often avoiding opening the post. If their husbands previously dealt with the bills they may have avoided conversations so that they were not reminded that they should not have been buying the amount of clothes or treats that they couldn't resist. Spenders find it difficult to budget and don't often plan for the future as the instant buzz they get from spending now is stronger than the need to feel in control of their money and look ahead. Some spenders spend to replace love or gain approval or "fit in". Some spend money on other people as well as themselves to increase the feeling of instant pleasure or to try to develop relationships.

Helpful tips for a spender

- A better route on the relationship side would be to try to build these on a basis other than money. Giving your time and effort to others may well be far more valuable to them and could be helpful for you to build your own self-worth.

- Reward yourself for something specific that you set yourself to do (not simply because you think you deserve it) and carry out the exercises in this book to help you gain a clear picture of your financial position.

- Leave your credit cards at home when you go shopping for a reward for yourself; decide on how much you're going to spend and then take that amount in cash. Make it a bit of a challenge to find something within that cash budget and it will have more impact when you hand over the actual money than simply keying in your pin number.

WORRIER

A worrier often has sleepless nights worrying about money, which can stem from different causes, for example lack of confidence, family dynamics such as parents with little money or partners who were frugal and criticised any spending. Often worriers suffer after having made a purchase or taking money decisions thinking that they've made a mistake, agonising on what they should have done differently especially when, as now, they are having to make these decisions on their own. Sometimes they become paralysed with fear about money issues, taking so long to make a decision, opportunities pass them by. Sometimes their thoughts and fears are totally irrational and completely consume them.

Helpful tips for a worrier

- Try writing down your worries and then outline what would be the worst that could actually happen. Do this whenever you feel really anxious and you may find seeing this laid out on paper helps you feel more in control.

- If you lie awake at night worrying use your note book to write down the things that are keeping you from sleeping and tell yourself that you will deal with the list the next day. Don't try and work them out in the middle of the night, just try and park them if you can so you can get some rest.

- Try not to constantly look at your finances, just do it properly once a month when you have the foundations of your budgeting and financial planning in place as I have shown you how to do already, perhaps having a set day or two each month to really focus on it.

- Try paying your bills by direct debit so that you know it will happen without your involvement.

- If you can, train yourself not to think about money constantly. Give yourself permission to put it out of your mind, and the rest of the time, allow yourself to concentrate on other things.

Having looked at these descriptions, think about how you relate to money:

- Are you a spender or a saver?
- Do you live like a church mouse with plenty of money in the bank?
- Do you have a lot of credit card debt?

- Do you give away too much money to your children?

You may recognise yourself in one or more of these money personalities and in fact you may have had a different style before the loss of your husband. You may also recognise your husband in some of the descriptions and that will be helpful too, as this may have influenced the way you think about money.

Think about

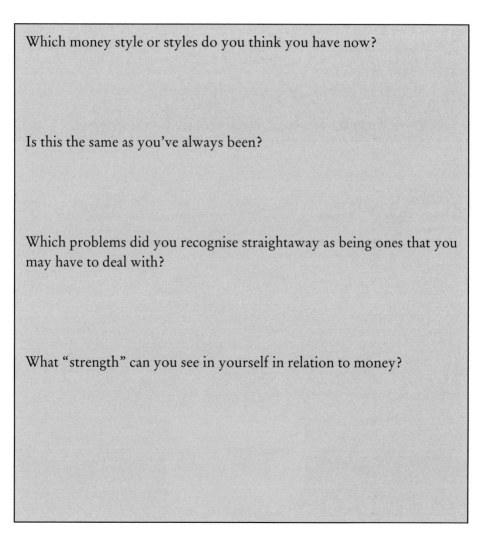

Which money style or styles do you think you have now?

Is this the same as you've always been?

Which problems did you recognise straightaway as being ones that you may have to deal with?

What "strength" can you see in yourself in relation to money?

We often hold onto beliefs without realising we have them or why we have them and so it is useful to know yourself better. This will help you to recognise your natural inclinations toward spending, saving, giving and investing.

Being more honest with yourself and having a better understanding of how you feel around money will help you to take control and make the changes that will create the financial plans and organisation that is best for you now that you are going to be managing your own finances.

6

Getting to grips with tax

"Fall seven times, stand up eight"

Japanese Proverb

*I*t is really important to understand the basics of **how tax works** so you can make your money work harder. Let's make a start and I'll show you some information to give you help in understanding how the tax system works in areas that might affect you. I am not going to cover everything – at this stage you just need to get the picture in your mind.

It will be *really* useful, so stick with it, but I would now make yourself a strong cup of tea to help you digest it.

Try this

As you read through this chapter jot down some of the important points in your note book, as writing down information can sometimes make it clearer in your own mind.

Understanding how your interest is taxed

We'll begin by looking at the way building society and bank interest is taxed as it is important for you to understand this when we think about the best ways to try to make the most of your capital.

Before a bank or building society pays you the interest on your deposit account, they will pay the tax man 20% of your interest and give you the rest. It is a clever way for the tax man not to have to do the work of collecting it himself. So, when you see the interest rate advertised, for example at 3% **gross** this means this is the rate before the building society takes off the tax they have to pay to tax man.

You are then left with the **net** interest of 2.4% which the building society will add to your account.

Look at the picture below. It shows how this would work in practice:

If you are a non-tax payer you can fill in an R85 tax form, which your building society will give you, and they can then pay you all the interest and nothing to the tax man. I'll show you later in this chapter how to see if you are a non-tax payer.

The importance of income tax on your money flow

Think of the tax man looking at how much each person earns, like having a jug with a name on it that he will use as a measure.

Think of your jug with your name; any salary, bonus or pension, interest or other income you receive, goes into this measuring jug and, depending on where the level comes up to, will show what kind of tax payer you are.

Generally, the amount you can earn without having to pay tax, known as your **personal allowance**, goes up each year, changing on 6th April, the start of the new tax year.

As our example, I am using the figures for April 6th 2013 to April 5th 2014, the dates that make up the tax year. Bear in mind that these figures will change each year on 6th April and this example is just to explain in principle how the system works. It doesn't cover all aspects of income tax, but it will be a useful visual to keep in your mind.

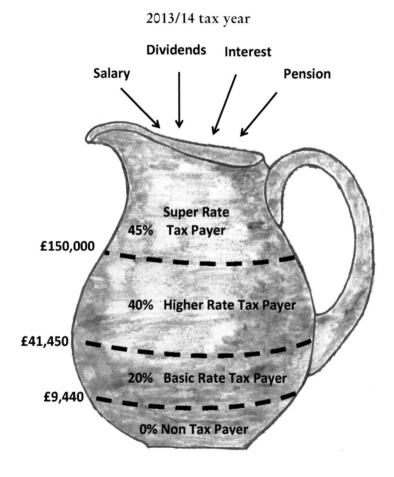

2013/14 tax year

If you have less than £9,440 in income from your earnings *and* your savings, you will be sitting within the first level of the jug, known as your **personal**

allowance, and will be a **non tax payer.** If part of this income is from interest on building society accounts and tax has been taken off your interest you will be able to claim this back.

If you use up your personal allowance and then have only a modest amount of savings interest, up to £2,790 in the 2013/4 tax year, there is a lower rate of tax just for savings interest in this narrow band. This slice should be only taxed at 10%, not 20%, and you can reclaim from the tax man the 10% of overpaid tax that the bank has paid to him.

If when added together your earnings and gross savings interest puts you into the 40% measure, above £41,450, you will need to pay some extra tax to the tax man on the interest that you have already received from your building society savings. This is because he wants 40% and you have only paid 20% through the building society. If you fall into this category, a higher rate tax payer, financial advice is likely to be very useful.

If your total income takes you above £100,000, then your personal allowance, the first measure of £9,440 at the bottom of your jug, begins to be reduced bit by bit so that once you are earning more than £118,880 you have no personal allowance, leaving you no band at all that is tax free. If you fall into this category you would definitely benefit from talking to a financial planner who could look at your income and work out if you can arrange your financial affairs so that you don't lose your slice on which you pay no tax at all.

If you earn more than £150,000 a year, currently, you will pay 45% on the slice of your income over that measure. This would make you an "additional" rate tax payer but I have called it super rate as it's more descriptive.

Your salary or pension income is normally taxed at the correct rate before you receive it, but as we've seen, interest from deposit accounts is only taxed at 20% because the building society take it off you and send it to the tax man not knowing whether this is the right amount or not as they don't know what other income you have. If you pay higher rates of tax the tax man will want you to send a payment to him to make up the difference and will tell you the amount he wants based on your tax return. Not everyone is sent a tax return so don't worry if you don't receive one. If you think you might owe the taxman money or you think that he owes you some give the helpline a ring on 0845 300 0627. They will need your National Insurance number so make sure you have it before you ring.

As for a 40% tax payer, a 45% tax payer would be wise to take some expert advice.

Age allowance for tax

If you are already 65, instead of the ordinary personal allowance you have something called Age Allowance, which allows you to earn more income before you start to pay tax. If you are over 75 there is another increase to the allowance. However, if when you add up your income from all your different sources it comes to more than £26,100 in 2013/14, the tax man starts to knock off some of this extra allowance until, if you are earning £28,220 a year, you are back to having the same personal allowance as everyone else under the age of 65. Income from ISAs does not count in the totting up so can be very useful (I will cover ISAs in Chapter 9).

However, the Chancellor Mr Osborne recently announced two significant changes

* First, while the personal allowance for the under 65s increased again in April 2013 to £9,440, the allowance for those aged 65 and over was frozen at the same levels as 2012-13.

* Secondly, anyone who turns 65 after 5 April 2013, does not get an extra allowance at all. They will benefit from the same personal allowance as the under-65s.

If you are over 65 with an income of more than £28,220, you are not affected at all, because you would not have received the extra allowance anyway.

Overpaying tax

If your income is below the personal allowance line on your jug, you can check your figures using the tax man's calculator on the government website, and you should be able to receive your interest without any tax being taken off. www.hmrc.gov.uk/calcs/r85/

By filling in an R85 form and giving it to your bank or building society, you will then be able to change your accounts so that you receive all the interest. Your bank will have a supply of these forms or you can download one from the Internet.

If you have been paying tax on your interest for some time and should not have been, then you are due for a refund. By filling in an R40 claim form, you will be able to claim this back. www.hmrc.gov.uk/tdsi/claim-tax-back.htm

If you should have only paid 10% tax on your building society interest instead of the 20% that is sent automatically to the tax man, you can use the same form to request a refund.

Underpaying tax

You and your husband may have split your money held in banks or building societies between you so that you could receive your interest without paying tax if you had very little other income being paid to you in your name. As it will all be in just your name now, you need to look at this again and, if necessary, make sure that you tell the building society or bank that you need to start paying tax on your interest so that you don't end up with an unwelcome, unexpected tax bill sometime in the future. It is always best to sort out your tax position so that it is correct as quickly as possible.

This section is not, of course, trying to show you the exact way that the whole income tax system works, there is more to it and it can be very complex *but* I do want you to have an idea of what it looks like and how you fit into it in broad terms. If you think that you have paid too much tax or are likely to pay too little then contact the taxman (details in the resources section of this book), an accountant or a financial planner.

Capital gains and capital gains tax (CGT)

One of the other taxes that you may need to know about is Capital Gains Tax (CGT). This is a completely different tax to Income Tax. This is a tax that you need to be aware of if you "dispose" of some types of assets such as a holiday home or stocks and shares. A **disposal** is the technical word that covers selling, giving away or transferring your asset, in other words if it no longer belongs to you. It is important to understand whether you need to pay any CGT if you decide to do something with your assets. For example if you inherited some stocks and shares and then some time later you sold them for more than they were worth when you inherited them, then you have made a profit known as a **capital gain**.

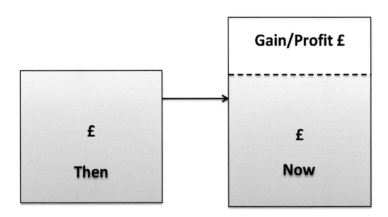

This "disposal", in other words the sale of the stocks and shares, might mean you will have a tax bill on the profit that you make. This profit is known as a "gain" by the taxman, so either word means the same thing.

Each tax year you have a Capital Gains Tax allowance, known as the *annual exempt amount*, which is the amount of profit you are allowed to make from disposing of assets in each tax year without having to pay any tax. Capital gains tax is often abbreviated to CGT.

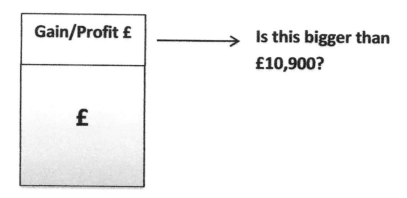

For the tax year 2013/14, the allowance is £10,900. This figure usually goes up each tax year.

Taking our example, let's say you inherited some stocks and shares worth £40,000 and you decided later that you wanted to sell them and you went ahead and sold them for £50,000. Your profit, also known as your gain, would be £10,000.

Because this profit is less than the £10,900 the tax man says you can make tax free, it is within your allowance and you would have no tax to pay.

So what would happen if you sold them for £60,000 and made more profit? Your profit would then be £20,000. This is above your allowance of £10,900 by £9,100.

This amount of £9,100, the **taxable** profit you have made, is added to your income tax jug for the tax man to work out which of the two different tax rates for CGT you will have to pay.

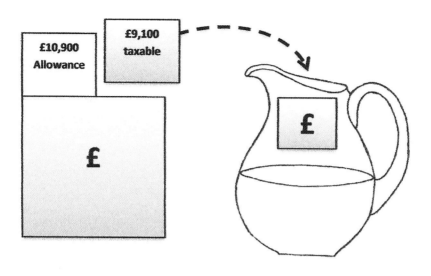

Does your taxable profit when it's added to your income in your jug take your level above the basic rate tax line into the higher rate tax band? If it all stays below the line, your capital gains tax bill will be 18% of your taxable profit on your shares.

If your level now goes above that basic rate tax line, whatever sits above in the higher income tax rate level is taxed at 28%. So in some situations you may have some of your profit taxed at 18% and some at 28%. If you are a higher rate tax payer or super rate tax payer already you will pay 28% on all the taxable profit.

If, on the other hand, you make a loss on an asset, you can normally use this loss to reduce any gain on other assets that you sell for a profit. This reduces the amount of tax you might have to pay. If you don't have any gains to match against the loss, you can carry it forward into the future to use at another time.

Your Capital Gains Tax allowance is an important allowance that many people, including some financial advisers, either ignore, forget or don't know about. It might be very useful when you consider how you might invest for your future to think not just about investments that are income tax efficient but also ones that would make profits that you can use for your CGT allowance too.

Try this

If you have details of your income now, use the measuring jug below to see how your own income level looks so that you will have an idea of any action you might need to take.

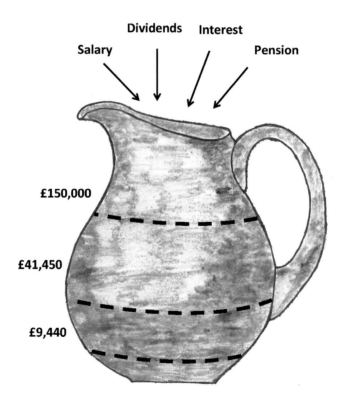

Are you paying too much tax on your savings?

Do you need to contact the tax office to check what to do?

Do you have assets that you or your husband have bought in the past that you might want or need to sell?

Do you know how much you paid for those assets so you can roughly work out whether you might have to pay tax?

I think that you need a break from tax now, so I have covered Inheritance Tax in the chapter called "Putting your house in order" as too much tax talk is taxing, but it is useful to understand some of the basics.

7

Keeping Investing Simple

"All things are difficult before they are easy"

Thomas Fuller

I want to take a look now at some useful facts that will help you to consider whether you should be making some investments as part of your financial planning. Perhaps you are thinking why bother with investing. It might seem unnecessary to you. After all, you have some money in the building society and that is earning interest. The problem we all face in relation to our money is *inflation* and the effect it has on its value.

Let's look back to 1985. Why, you might ask? Well, it's far enough back that it will serve the purpose, yet not so long ago that we can't relate to it.

• In the charts Madonna was singing "Crazy for You" and Dire Straits were up there with "Money for Nothing"

• At the cinema we were going to see "A View to a Kill" and "Mad Max Beyond Thunderdome"

• We watched as Boris Becker became the youngest winner of the men's Wimbledon championships

It does not seem that long ago to me, but maybe that's my age.

However, what *does* seem a long time ago are the prices at that time.

• Average House Price £40,169
• Litre of Petrol 42p
• 1lb tomatoes 49p
• 1lb potatoes 10p
• 1 pint milk 20p
• 10 fish fingers 85p
  Figures from BBC *Domesday Reloaded*

We can see from this how inflation has changed the price of goods we need to buy, but how does inflation impact on our capital?

It means our capital's spending power decreases unless you can keep its value moving ahead by the same level as inflation. Back in 1985 if you had £10,000 you would need to have grown it to £25,300 to have the same spending power now as then. The number is bigger but it would only buy the same amount of goods. This is significant as, according to the Office for National Statistics, the average life expectancy for most women in the UK will be around 82, unless you live in Kensington where it rises to 89!

By understanding this, you will be able to look differently at how to make the most of your money and what to do with it. Think about it this way:

If inflation is 4% a year your capital needs to grow by 4% a year, no matter where it is invested, just to hold its spending power and so stand still.

Bearing in mind the need to try to maintain your money's value, sensible investing is so important. You may never have made any investments or you may have inherited investments from your husband. He may have made investments for you or you may have a range of investments that you have made yourself already.

I want to either change the way that you think about investing if you already have some investments or, if you've not yet made any investment decisions, I would like you to have some useful knowledge before you consider taking any action.

I'd like to tell you about Barbara, one of my clients, as I think her story will help me explain some of the areas that I believe are important about investing for you.

Barbara's story

Barbara's husband, Peter, throughout his lifetime loved to "play" the stock market and had, during their marriage together, bought many different investments in both his name and Barbara's. She took absolutely no interest in them whatsoever, making sure that when they had conversations around his love of investing, she made the right noises at the right time but basically left him to it. He spent hours reading the financial pages of the newspapers, reading "The Economist" and talking to his stockbroker who looked after some of their investments. Peter's study was full of paperwork going back many years and Barbara didn't even like going in there to vacuum as she always felt so overwhelmed just by the look of it all.

After Peter died unexpectedly, one of the biggest fears Barbara had to face was the thought of having to take over the responsibility of their investments. Peter had left a very good list of the investments they both held but it could have been written in Japanese for all it meant to Barbara.

Barbara's solicitor suggested that she meet with me to help decide which of Peter's assets she should transfer into her own name and keep and which she should sell. So we began the process, exactly like the one I have shown you in Chapter 2, looking at what she had coming in, what was going out, and what she had in her tank as, until we knew that, no decisions could be made. Barbara also needed to boost her own confidence, building her own knowledge around what she now had, and to create her own system so she knew where she was.

We quickly realised that she was fortunate that she had a good level of income to cover her outgoings and that she did not need to make any snap decisions.

We talked about Peter's love of investing and I asked questions about how he made his mind up about the investments he bought. Peter used

to look for shares on the stockmarket or funds (a collection of different shares managed by an investment fund manager I will cover these in Chapter 8) that had been performing well and that were popular with the financial press.

Barbara told me that there were times when Peter was very anxious about some of their investments, selling them after they had gone down because he was worried that they would go down further. Sometimes he told her he was holding onto investments, saying he was waiting until they came back up in value to the same price that he had paid for them, and then he would be selling them. She said he was always feeling that he should be doing something, not wanting to miss out or make a mistake, sometimes appearing very unsure of what to do but then at other times, he seemed very confident in either his own decision-making or in other people's opinions in the financial pages of the newspapers. How would she ever be able to manage all of this with the enormous pressures it all seemed to bring and the contradictions and complexities that even Peter sometimes struggled with?

Helping Barbara to see her position, the next step we took was to carefully look at all the investments she now owned that Peter had chosen. Using some specialist software, we shook them up together and then separated them out to see them in a different way. We grouped them into the same categories; for example all investments that sat in UK shares were added up, all those in European shares and so on.

What Barbara was able to see when we did this, was that there was a heavy concentration of funds that looked different to each other but were actually buying the same underlying investments. This meant that there was a higher level of risk than if they had been more spread out; lots of eggs in one basket!

I asked Barbara if she thought Peter had had an overall plan that related to their lives when he was making his investments and her answer was that she felt he might have enjoyed the feeling of having a "flutter" rather than having a plan for their money.

We talked about the wisdom of not having all eggs in one basket and about the fact that no one actually knows which investment will be the most successful in the future, that there are no fancy secrets. The gurus writing in the papers don't know either. If it's in print for millions to read, it certainly is no secret and if they really knew they would be on an exotic island counting their money!

The reality was that Peter never had to choose the perfect investment, no one can, but there are millions of pounds spent each year trying to convince us that it is possible!

It's a wild goose chase.

> "What is quite remarkable in the investment world is that people are playing a game which in some sense cannot be played.
>
> There are so many people out there in the market: the idea that any individual without extra information or extra market power can beat the market is extraordinarily unlikely. And yet the market is full of people who think they can do it and full of other people who believe them.
>
> This is one of the great mysteries of finance: why do people believe they can do the impossible?
>
> And why do people believe them?"
>
> Daniel Kahneman, Professor of Psychology and Public Affairs, Princeton University and 2002 Nobel Prize Winner

I explained to Barbara that investing is a little like the Tortoise and the Hare; slow and steady is likely to win the race. Peter had been wearing himself out with plenty of busy activity like the hare and, up until that point, Barbara thought that was how it was.

No wonder she was filled with dread, thinking she would have to somehow do the same, but on her own. The fact is that markets are unpredictable. The truth is that it is very difficult for anyone, fund managers and stockbrokers included, to move out of investments at the right time into cash and back in again. Or to identify the next Microsoft or Apple and buy shares in that company before they become household names.

Looking for these gurus, these top performing managers quoted in the money pages in the weekend newspapers, is fraught with danger as you are assessing their skill on how they have fared in the past.

Can you tell if it was luck or judgement? It's easy to say "There's a great horse" after it has won the race.

Here is the most illuminating idea – you don't need to try and beat the returns that the world's stockmarkets will provide you. Over the medium to long term, simply by capturing the returns that the markets will deliver by using low cost index funds, you are likely to do better than most, without the anxiety that can come with worrying about whether your fund manager is worth his salt.

Investment is not winning or losing, no one takes all the spoils leaving nothing for the rest and so, by understanding the truth of this, you will receive your fair share of the profits by putting some of your money to work in the global economy.

Instead of trying to time the market or pick winning fund managers before they have had their run of good performance, a more reliable approach is to invest broadly in a large spread of a particular asset class, accepting the return this will bring. This is also known as indexing, and is generally a cheaper way to invest money as there are lower costs linked to running these types of funds.

The way I believe investments should work, is for each one to have its place and be there for a reason and purpose, a bit like a piece in a patchwork or an ingredient in a recipe.

In their case, Peter had been collecting random pieces because they looked and sounded good but, in truth, were disjointed. So, we discussed the importance of making sure that we simplified Barbara's finances so that she felt confident about the ingredients that were important for her, looked at her tax position and reflected what she was going to need in her life.

Barbara is a marvellous gardener and so we talked in terms of planning what was needed, preparing the ground, getting rid of what would not fit in the design stage, using the right elements, not paying more in costs than necessary and then letting the whole thing grow undisturbed, not moving stuff around constantly for the sake of it, checking progress and fine tuning and pruning each year.

The relief she felt in realising that she could approach things differently from Peter was enormous and she now runs her finances in a simple and effective way, only spending the time she needs to on it, meeting with me to make sure she is on track each year, preferring to spend her time in her magnificent garden and with her friends and family.

Some of the things I was able to explain to Barbara about investing are really only common sense but there is so much mystique and jargon around the subject that it is hard to see the wood for the trees. I have come to the conclusion, after nearly thirty years in the investment world, that there is quite a lot of pontificating which often is just "noise".

But unless someone helps you to see it differently why would you doubt how it all appears to work?

I believe that it's important to use facts rather than believe marketing hype. This is more likely to deliver a better investment outcome, helping you make smarter, informed choices around your investment planning.

Let's look at some of these next.

8

Investment Nuts and Bolts

"If you don't like something, change it; if you can't change it, change the way you think about it."

Mary Engelbreit

*L*et's look at some of the nuts and bolts around investing and gather some facts as we do so. You may be in a position where you feel you do not need to invest any money but, if you need your capital to keep pace with inflation for the rest of your lifetime, good tax planning and proper investment planning are the two strategies that will give you the best chance of succeeding in this.

This part of the book might be the hardest to digest and it would be a good idea if you read it again once you start to focus on what you might do or after you have spoken to someone about investment. You will find that you begin to fit the financial jigsaw pieces into place and it will start to make more sense.

So let's look at two of the first lessons in investing, the type of things you can typically invest in and the types of risk that might affect these investments.

Understanding different investment risks

To understand risk you need to know that, in basic terms, there are four main areas, also known as **asset classes**, where you can invest or deposit money:

- Cash
- Fixed Interest
- Property
- Shares

We'll look at these in more detail later in this chapter but for now we need to know their names as they carry different kinds of risk and are likely to give you different potential returns.

Different kinds of risk

We'll now look at risks that you need to be aware of, so when you start to make decisions about your financial situation, you are more likely to be able to ask the right questions and make informed choices. There are four different kinds of risk:

- Capital risk
- Liquidity risk
- Income or shortfall risk
- Institutional risk

CAPITAL RISK

The picture below lines up the four asset classes against each other on a scale of risk and potential rewards.

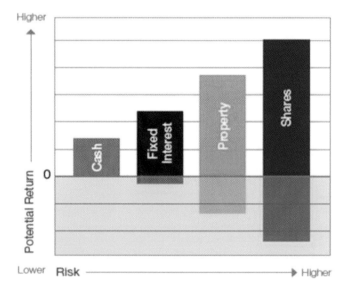

As you can see from the diagram, cash sits at the lower end in terms of both risk and returns, with shares at the other, higher end of the scale. Now this is the traditional view of risk because this scale uses the chance of your capital *going down* in value as the barometer, and this is known as **capital risk**. This is also known as **volatility**, the movement of something's value going up and down.

A proportion of your money might stay invested for many years or even the rest of your life, to be passed on to your family. The longer your investment horizon, the more you are able to ride out any movements in the value of some of your investments. Notice that I said "some". This is back to not having all your eggs in one basket.

LIQUIDITY RISK

Another risk is liquidity risk, which is the danger of not being able to get at your money when you need it. For example, if you invest in a fixed-term savings scheme, you might not be able to take out your money until the end of this period. There may be a financial penalty for taking it out early. With some investments it's difficult to get at your money quickly.

Or, if you buy another property as an investment, you won't be able to get at your cash until you've sold it, which might take months or even years. So making sure you have access to enough cash that is easily accessible for those unforeseen emergencies is really important.

INCOME OR SHORT-FALL RISK

This is the risk that returns from your savings or investments will be less than you expect. Think of how low interest rates have been in recent times. If you have a mortgage, low interest rates are good, but if you rely on the interest from your bank or building society for some of your income, over the last ten or so years you will have seen your income drop significantly.

INSTITUTIONAL RISK

You need to think about the financial strength of the institution you save with. Once again, not having all your eggs in one basket is sensible but you don't have to overdo it and spread your cash deposits too thinly into small amounts, that just adds paperwork and makes it more difficult to keep on top of what you have. The savings safety net – otherwise known as the Financial Services Compensation Scheme (FSCS) – should protect you against a bank in the UK going bump. As I write this: in 2013 the compensation limit is £85,000 for each bank or building society you hold accounts with.

So, if a bank collapsed, you would be paid up to £85,000, but if the capital you have deposited is more than this amount then you won't get it all back.

With all the mergers and takeovers that have gone on over the last few years there is a possible trap that you might fall into. If any of your different banks or building societies sit under the same banking license, you will have just one lot of £85,000 covered, even though you think they are all different. You can check this by looking on the Internet for a list of banking licenses or phone your bank and ask them if your other account or accounts come under the same license.

A word of warning, the banks and building societies sometimes offer investments that sound like just another type of deposit account but actually, they aren't. These are known technically as **structured products** and typically have names such as "Capital Secure" or "Guaranteed Growth Plan" and are often sold to cautious investors looking for a better return than their deposit accounts. Make sure that you ask if the investment is covered by the FSCS and ask for the bank or building society to confirm that in writing.

So, as we have seen, there are several types of risk, the common denominator being uncertainty of future results.

Generally speaking, risk can be inflation eroding the value of your capital and income, a downturn in the stock market, interest rates moving up or down, the risk of living too long and running out of money and so on, not just some of your capital falling in value at some point.

Having looked at some of the risks, don't be put off finding out about investing. As I have said before, for many widows their biggest risk is money not keeping up with inflation and cash deposits often just don't cut the mustard.

The nuts and bolts of asset classes

Let's look now in more detail at the asset classes, the actual areas in which you can invest your money. This section will give you an idea of what the asset classes are.

SHARES

I'll start with **company shares**.

Shares are bought and sold on a stock market; there are stock markets for example in the UK, America, Hong Kong, Australia and so on. A share is also known as an **equity**. The stock market and the equity market are the same thing.

You also have equity in your own home if you own it.

So, equity is another name for a stake in something. With company shares, you own a stake in that particular business, having invested some of your money in exchange for two possible ways in which you can be rewarded.

The first is that you hope, when you sell your share that the price compared with the price you originally paid for it has gone up. You would then make a profit on the amount you invested in the first place. Of course, the reverse can and does happen, where you might get back less than you paid.

The second way owning a share can repay you for having a stake in the business, is by giving you a slice of some of their profits if they are doing well and have made enough money in the year. This is known as a **dividend**. The company "declares" or announces how much it will be paying out and then, for each share you own, you will receive that amount. As sometimes happens, if the company is going through difficult times, it may decide that it can't pay a dividend.

When a company pays you a dividend it is automatically taxed at 10% and you will receive 90% of the dividend income. The tax taken is known as the tax credit. The dividend you receive added to the tax credit equals the gross dividend.

Basic-rate taxpayers don't have to pay any more tax than the 10% that has already been paid before they receive this income but 40% and 45% tax payers do through their tax returns.

Share-based investments involve some risk as returns depend on how well the companies you own shares in perform, the performance of the stock market and the economy as a whole. It may be useful to know a bit more about some of the terminology you might come across.

There is a measure that you will have heard of that acts like a barometer for the UK stock market called the FTSE 100, known as the "Footsie". Simply put, the FTSE 100 is a measure, also known as an **index**, made up of the *100 largest* companies' shares listed on the London Stock Exchange. The index is seen, traditionally, as a good indication of the performance of major companies listed in the UK. The *FTSE All Share Index* tracks most of the shares on the London Stock Exchange rather than just the largest 100.

The other world stock markets have their own "indexes" which act as barometers for companies based there.

You may come across the term **benchmark**, which is another word in the investment world for a measure or comparison. Often an index is used as a benchmark to compare how an investment is doing against, say, the UK stockmarket.

If the stock market in general goes down due to economic uncertainty, the value of your shares may also fall, even if the company you hold shares in is doing well. If a particular type of company really suffers from difficult times, and you hold lots of shares in this sector (such as bank shares during the credit crunch) this can expose you to significant risk. So, it makes sense to reduce the risk of owning shares by owning shares of *different* types, for example oil companies, retailers and drugs companies, rather than concentrating on just one of these.

One client came to me with a share portfolio packed with bank shares she had inherited from her late husband before the credit crunch. Fortunately, we were able to sell most of these and invest in a really well-spread range, also known as a **diversified** range of investments, which meant that, when the credit crunch hit, she was not exposed to such a bumpy ride during that time.

Looking at further diversification, in these days of a global economy, owning shares in companies around the world makes more sense than just thinking about the UK. How many times have we seen news about jobs and business being lost to other parts of the world?

You can own actual shares directly or you can, instead, invest in an investment **fund** such as a **unit trust** or an open-ended investment company (**OEIC**) which own lots of different shares. I will explain later what these are.

PROPERTY

Although you might own your own property, investing into property as an asset class is different. This includes investment property such as property you buy to rent out (buy-to-let) and **property funds** such as unit trusts, OEICs or real estate investment trusts (**REITS**) which invest in commercial property such as offices, shopping centres and factories.

You can usually sell property investment funds much more quickly than buy-to-let property. However, it may be difficult to get at your money quickly if the investment fund invests in a range of bricks and mortar buildings and the investment manager has to sell actual properties to repay your capital. Some property investment funds have the right to delay payment by up to six months to give them time to sell properties if necessary. Some property funds invest in shares of property companies and are less likely to restrict you in getting your money out quickly. However, the day to day valuation may fluctuate more widely.

Property funds can go up and down in value so there is some capital risk, but they can be useful as part of a diversified portfolio as there is the possibility of both income and capital growth over time and they don't necessarily follow what happens in the stock market.

FIXED INTEREST BONDS

This includes **government bonds**, which are government borrowing from investors. These are also known as **gilts**. This shortened name, gilt, is because originally the piece of paper issued to an investor in exchange for their money going to the government, had a gilded edge and so was known as a gilt-edge security. It is thought that these first came about to fund the war with France in the 17th century.

So, when you buy gilts you are effectively lending the government money. In return, you usually receive a **fixed income** twice a year until the gilt matures. On maturity, you get back the nominal value of the gilt. This is the amount the gilt was originally sold for when it was first issued, but may be different from the price it was bought for. Gilts continue to be bought and sold after they have been issued in a second hand market, where institutions buy and sell in a way similar to the stock market and the price of the gilts changes as interest rates move and demand ebbs and flows.

There are also **index linked gilts**, which, as the name suggests, track inflation rates instead of being a fixed rate of interest.

As these investments need some research, many people will buy a fund holding different gilts maturing at different times with different interest rates, chosen by a fund manager rather than choosing which gilts to buy themselves.

Government bonds are attractive for a portion of most portfolios as they are considered more secure and less volatile than equities, creating a useful, steadier addition into the mix.

Corporate bonds are similar but, instead of being issued by the government, they are issued by companies or corporations when they want to raise money. As you would imagine, there are differences between the quality of the corporate bonds that are issued depending on how strong the business is that wants to raise the money. Think of the difference between, say, Marks and Spencer and a small local chain of food stores. The companies issuing corporate bonds, are measured by credit rating agencies, the strongest labelled as AAA, with a sliding scale as the companies reduce in investment quality. You may hear the term "Triple A rated" as a measure.

Good quality corporate bonds tend to be less volatile than shares so, like Government gilts, can add a useful more stable addition to a portfolio. Think diversification again, not all eggs in one basket.

As with shares, building a portfolio of corporate bonds requires skill and so most people prefer to invest in a ready-made portfolio, such as a corporate bond unit trust or OEIC.

These funds pool together investors' money and invest in lots of bonds or gilts so there is no single maturity date for your investment. Instead, you can choose when to sell (liquidate) your **units**, the description of the portion of that fund that you own.

The main risk with fixed interest investments is that the company or government might fail to return your capital, or not pay the interest promised, but these investments are generally regarded as lower risk than shares or property.

CASH ON DEPOSIT

We have already looked at cash on deposit with banks and building societies in ordinary deposit accounts. We looked at the way in which money held there is taxed and how it is important to make sure you don't forget to keep an eye on your cash deposit accounts. Keeping some easily accessible money on deposit for emergencies is a sensible plan.

Asset allocation

So, we've looked at the main asset classes, and next is how to blend them together. This is known as **asset allocation**, how big the slice of the pie for type of investment is.

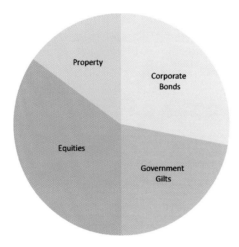

Sometimes, cash and fixed interest are grouped together and described as "Defensive" and property and shares grouped together and described as "Growth" and the mix of these is a common way of describing the blend. For example a 50/50 portfolio would be made up of half defensive and half growth elements.

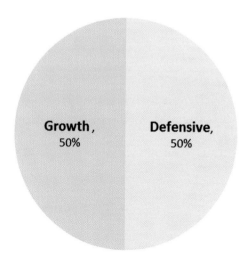

Working out what mix of these asset classes might be right for you is where an independent financial planner can help.

I don't think it is advisable to try and create your own mix of investments but by having some of these basic facts about how investing works, when someone perhaps suggests a mix, you will have more of an idea of what it means.

Sometimes the mix might be described in a different way, such as a **balanced** fund. Ask to be shown what the asset allocation is so that, using the descriptions above, you can gauge a bit better how the recipe looks.

The best mix for you will depend on two main things: your attitude to risk and secondly what you need your capital to achieve.

Your attitude to risk

More money has been lost by lack of remaining steady (people panicking and moving things around) than stock market movements. By staying the course, and keeping the portion of your investments in the assets that over time are most likely to beat inflation, you are more likely to make your investing more profitable. It is of course difficult, when watching the news broadcasting how dire everything is, not to panic and think that you need to move your money under the bed but, by remaining disciplined, you are much more likely to reap the rewards.

Perhaps by thinking of your capital as a cupboard with shelves might help. Imagine that you have different shelves on which you are going to put your money. The bottom shelf would be money sitting in your current account where you pay your bills.

The next shelf up would be a shelf with money on deposit with a bank or building society that you can easily move down to the current account below when you need to.

The next shelf up would be Cash ISAs, you would only use these if the next shelf down was empty as these make more money for you because you are not paying tax on the interest.

Above this would be a shelf with shares, gilts, bonds etc.

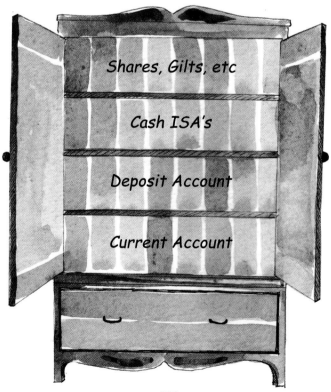

By imagining this picture, if your investments on the top shelf go down in value, remember that you have tucked them away at the top of the cupboard and ideally they should be there for a few years so that they can grow in value over time. A drop in their value should not be a reason to panic and liquidate them. Over time the value can change and investing is definitely not a sprint, it is more like a marathon.

Ideally, when faced with negative news on the television and bad news stories in the papers, you need to be able to tune out the noise, as I've mentioned before. Focus on things you can control, don't focus on such things you can't.

Diana rang me after she had seen coverage of the Japanese tsunami in 2010 wondering how this disaster was going to affect her investments. I explained to her that, first, this wasn't going to have a major effect on her money and, secondly, there was not a thing she or I could do to influence events in Japan. Based on this she should not be worrying herself about it in relation to her investments.

It was of course a tragedy, but one of many that occur every day on the planet. I, however, understood she just needed reassurance and after we had talked for a while, she suggested that she would limit the amount of news she would watch as it made her anxious.

As it turned out, once she got out of the habit of watching the news she said she felt much better about life in general, as she wasn't taking on her shoulders the world's problems, and that she had reduced wasting time or energy on the wrong things. It is interesting that one of the descriptions of the idyllic tranquil holiday destination of the Maldives is "No news, no shoes!" Perfect! No one has unlimited amounts of time or energy and especially during the difficult times you are having to deal with, reducing the amount of even sub conscious stress is a good strategy.

So don't derail yourself by being drawn in to worry about things you simply can't influence. Use your energy to focus and learn about the areas you can control, such as understanding what you have, minimising the amount of tax you need to pay, and how best to use your resources.

FIND OUT YOUR RISK PROFILE

There are some excellent risk profiling tests available to financial planners that can enable them to help you to get a feel for your own risk profile and help the adviser assess how you feel about and react to risk. These tests are usually a set of questions that have been tried out on a representative sample of the population. Based on the answers, the population is then divided into groups according to how much risk they seem to be comfortable with. When you take the test, your score is compared with the results for the population, which determines the risk group that seems the closest match to you. Don't panic thinking that you wouldn't have the right answers. These are multiple choice, not exam type questions, and there are no right or wrong answers, they are just a way to find out how you feel about different situations.

Although really useful, these tests won't give you an absolute measure of the amount of risk you are comfortable with or that you should take. But they will ask you interesting questions that might get you thinking about what you are comfortable with and what you are not.

What does your capital need to achieve?

The second important aspect to thinking about the right blend of investments for you is what does your capital need to achieve during your lifetime? Do you really need to drive it hard to make as much as possible?

Jennie came to me with a very racy investment portfolio that had been put together by a stockbroker and she was worried because she kept receiving masses of paperwork almost weekly that she didn't understand, and she had seen big fluctuations in the value of her portfolio. When we put together her "Money Flow" picture, I was able to tell her that she could reduce the riskiness of her invested money because her excellent index linked widow's pension from her husband's job, meant she simply didn't need to take so much risk. We simplified everything and reduced both her paperwork and her risk, as we agreed there was no need to drive her money that hard, she was going to have enough with low risk investments.

So, to recap, in this chapter we covered risks around investing and the different types of assets you can invest in. Next, I'll look at how you can actually make an investment and if you already have some this next chapter will help you understand them more.

9

Putting Your Money to Work

"If you have the courage to begin,
you have the courage to succeed"

David Viscott

This chapter will guide you further into the world of investments, increasing your knowledge about investing. Keep going even if it seems complicated, as the more you can understand bit by bit, the more likely you are to make sound investment decisions for your future.

Let's remind ourselves of the main asset classes:

- Shares
- Property
- Fixed interest bonds
- Cash on deposit

How do you invest in these asset classes?

Now that we have looked at the asset classes and the concept of **risk**, the next question is how do you buy your assets and "store" them.

STORAGE BAGS FOR ASSET CLASSES

I want you to think in terms of holding your asset classes in different storage bags. Here is a list of the names of typical storage bags that you might find you already have, or that might be useful for you to have in the future depending on your own circumstances. I will explain what each "bag" is and what it does in this chapter and I will show them as different pictures.

- Cash ISA

- Stocks and shares ISA

- Unit Trust / OIEC

- Onshore Investment Bond

- Offshore Investment Bond

- Pension

Let's go back to Barbara. I want to give you some more pictures to explain some of the types of investments Barbara found she had. The list of investments that Peter had left her, if you remember, was daunting and she was panicking, thinking it was all just too complicated. She actually had all of the investments I have listed above.

There are quite a few other storage bags that can hold asset classes inside them, more than Barbara's list, but I'll explain those she had as they are the ones you are most likely to either have yourself or hear about when taking some advice. It will be useful to understand the basics if you are considering making some investments, as some of these bags are likely to be recommended and re-reading this chapter at that time would be a good idea

Investment storage bags in detail

Each of these bags has a different set of tax rules attached to them and so, depending on your own particular situation, one bag might be better for you than another. This is why it is so important for you, or whoever you use to help you with your investments, to really understand your own tax position clearly, as I showed you in Chapter 6.

When you take advice or read any other information on investments, if you hear or see the term "wrapper", you just need to know this is another way of describing our bags.

In the list were Cash ISAs, let's use these to kick off as they are the simplest to start with. A Cash ISA is what I would describe as a storage bag, it's a bag to hold the invested money inside. In this case the bag, the Cash ISA, is designed to hold only *cash on deposit, no other asset class.*

Understanding cash ISAs

Let's look to see how cash Individual Savings Accounts (ISAs) might be useful. These are *deposit accounts* with banks and building societies where the tax man has agreed that you will *not* have to pay him any tax on the interest that the ISA account earns. So, the picture for a cash ISA in comparison to your normal building society or bank deposit account that we looked at in Chapter 6 looks like this; no sign of the tax man this time:

Now for the catch, but it is only a small one. You can only put a certain amount into a cash ISA each tax year, but you can open a second ISA in the next tax year and so on, each one sitting parallel to the others. You can choose a different bank or building society each year but remember that as soon as you put even £1 in an ISA in a tax year you can only add more money to that particular one, you can't open another that year.

A Widow's Guide

For the tax year running from 6th April 2012 to 5th April 2013 you can put a maximum amount of £5,640, known as your **allowance**, into a cash ISA, which will grow free of tax. This means it will be growing faster than a normal building society account paying the same interest rate.

Here's where your calendar will be needed again as part of your system. The best rates for building society accounts including cash ISAs often include a bonus for a period of normally twelve months. After that, the interest rate often goes down to a horribly low level. The trouble is that twelve months can go by so quickly, that you can miss the fact that the interest rate has already gone down. By putting a reminder in your calendar that you need to look at the savings rate you won't be caught out.

This is when you need to be prepared to move your money to make sure it's working hard for you. It might seem an obvious statement but I have known people who were afraid to move their money from one bank to another as they felt guilty moving it away. Don't forget it is yours not the building society's or the bank's! You're in charge of your money and if you get into good habits the pounds will mount up.

Have a look in the weekend papers as they often have a "best buy" list of cash ISAs, or look online with a site such as www.moneysupermarket.com. Make sure you check to see if there are any restrictions on being able to access your money if you need it.

If a bank or building society has a very good cash ISA when you come to choose one for the new tax year, ask if you can add (known as a **transfer**) your old ones into the new one at the same time. This will do two useful things for you.

First, you will be making sure more of your money is receiving a better interest rate and secondly it keeps your cash ISAs simpler to keep track of as, over the years, you might build up several. Keeping them nice and tidy and lumped together can work well.

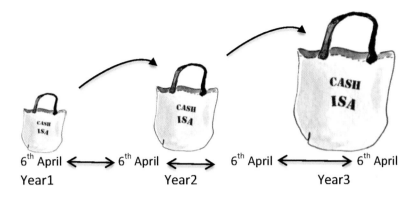

6th April ← → 6th April ← → 6th April ← → 6th April
Year1   Year2   Year3

If you are not in a position to keep using up your allowance, you should still look at the interest rate on your ISA each year and if there is another with a better rate you should think about moving it by "transferring". Doing this will not use up your allowance for the new tax year, it will still be there. The banks or building societies will move the money between themselves. It will happen behind the scenes once you have completed the forms.

Investment storage bags in detail

As its name suggests, the Cash ISA bag only holds cash. Let's think about the other bags. What some people find confusing is the difference between these bags and what actually goes inside them. Moreover, why have a particular bag.

You start by finding out what level of investment risk you would be comfortable with and how hard your money needs to work. This will allow a mix of asset classes to be blended together for you. The choice of which bag to use will depend on things that are relevant to you, such as what type of tax payer you are, how old you are, how much overall capital you have, whether your aim is to create income in retirement, whether you need to create income because you have already retired or whether you might want to make gifts to family, for example. So you might have several bags to do different jobs, but the investments bought inside are likely to be the same as this is based on your attitude to risk.

The important thing to remember about the bags is that there are advantages and disadvantages to each one and you may never have the need for some of them. A particular bag may be better for you than another.

Apart from the Cash ISA bag, the diversified mixture of the different asset classes that is right for you can go into every one of the bags. This mixture of ingredients is known as a **portfolio**. Each of our bags can contain a *portfolio* or mixture of the asset classes we looked at in Chapter 8, shares from companies around the world, gilts, corporate bonds and property investments.

Remember that the same mixture of asset classes can be held in every bag, so thinking about these two elements, the portfolio and the bag as different decisions should make it less confusing. Keep that in mind as I build the idea in pictures to help you see how the other bags work.

UNIT TRUSTS AND OEICS (Pronounced OYKS)

Unit trust   OEICS

Unit trusts and open-ended investment companies (OEICs) are very similar to each other and are investment funds, which pool together investors' money. This money is then invested by a **fund manager** into any of the main asset classes we have looked at. I have asked you to imagine our bags hold a mixture of those asset classes but you may already have some unit trusts which hold only one or two types. It will be helpful here to give you some examples. They might have names such as a "Japanese Smaller Companies Fund", which tells you that the fund manager who controls that bag's investment buys the shares of smaller companies on the Japanese Stock Market. A "UK Equity Fund" will be run by a fund manager who buys shares in UK companies. Sometimes the name of a fund doesn't describe clearly what it invests in but many do.

With a unit trust you buy units in the fund, and with an OEIC you buy shares. Both are open-ended funds, which means, when new money comes into the fund, the fund manager buys more assets, and new units or shares are created. The price of units and shares is determined by the value of the assets in the fund and will rise or fall in line with the value of those assets; prices are published daily in the press and on the Internet.

There are two ways that these bags can make you money. The first is income from the investments inside the bag and the second comes from the value of the units or shares you own going up in value so that, when you sell them, you hope to make more than you paid for them.

There are two taxes that you need to think about with these bags. Generally, income that appears in the bag from the investments will be taxable as if it were dividend income so non-tax payers won't be able to claim any tax back, basic rate tax payers won't have any more tax to pay and higher rate and super higher rate tax payers will have some extra income tax to pay.

The second tax is Capital Gains Tax (CGT). The good news though is you have a CGT allowance, at the time of writing of £10,900 for the year. This is a most underused tax allowance in my opinion. If you have used up your ISA allowance, as your most tax efficient shelf, and you still have more money that needs to be invested, using a unit trust or OEIC bag can be really useful. In the future, you could look at taking some profits out of the bag, aiming to use up some of your CGT allowance, meaning that any growth will have been tax free.

INDIVIDUAL SAVINGS ACCOUNTS (ISAs)

We've already looked at Cash ISAs, but here we are looking at Stocks and shares ISA's which are different as the contents of the bag are not just cash. Stocks and shares ISAs have the same structure as OEICS and Unit Trusts but with special tax treatment and so are made to look different and are labelled as ISAs so everyone knows they are to be treated differently. There is also a limit on how much can go in.

You can either choose to invest your whole allowance of £11,520 (2013/2014) into a stocks and shares ISA, or split it in two and invest up to half, £5,760, into each type.

Any income or profits from a stocks and shares ISA are tax-free. This means you don't have to pay income tax on any income that you actually receive or income that gathers inside the ISA. There is no capital gains tax to pay on any profits when you sell. If you are a higher rate taxpayer, stocks and shares ISAs will be very attractive as you will have to pay 40% tax on any income that comes to you from most other investments.

You can transfer from one stocks and shares ISA to another whenever you want. If it's an old ISA from previous years, you can transfer all or part of the value. If it's the current tax year's ISA you have to transfer everything you've paid in since the beginning of the tax year. You can only transfer money invested in a stocks and shares ISA into another stocks and shares ISA; to visualise this, think about the bag having to be the same. But, if you have money in a cash ISA this can be transferred into a stocks and shares ISA. Now the bag can change colour!

Try and keep your ISAs tidy and easy to keep track of by thinking about moving your cash ISAs to one with a really good rate each year, adding the new year's top up at the same time.

With your stocks and shares ISAs, try to find an adviser who can help you keep things simple and tidy. They can often recommend an ISA bag that can be added to each year to receive your allowance with no restriction on the choice of investments that you can hold inside it. This means you will just have one stocks and shares ISA bag, making the paperwork easier than having lots of separate smaller ones. If you do this and use your allowance each year, the ISA bag will grow in size and will appear to be bigger than you are allowed but you will have only invested the same amount as someone with several smaller bags.

ONSHORE INVESTMENT BONDS

It is a bit confusing that a **bond,** as well as being an asset class (ie the corporate and government fixed interest bonds we have already looked at) is also the name of a bag or wrapper. These bags are known as **single premium investment bonds, insurance bonds** or **life assurance bonds.** Although these names seem different they are all basically the same bag. These bags can have fixed interest bonds, together with the other asset classes sitting inside them, which can be hard to understand. A bond inside a bond, two different things!

There are two main investment bond bags, **onshore** and **offshore**.

An **onshore investment bond** is normally offered by a life insurance company and is based here in the UK. There are several variations, such as **distribution bonds, high-income bonds** and **with-profits bonds**, with the names describing what is sitting inside the bags.

As life policies, onshore investment bonds are taxed in a particular way. The insurance company that creates the bag is responsible for paying tax on the income and profits made by the investments inside it. You can't reclaim any of this tax even if you are a non tax payer. This means that people who pay income tax at the basic rate or less, or don't use their capital gains tax allowance, may get a better return by choosing a different bag, such as ISAs or Unit Trusts and OEICS.

Because the insurance company has already paid tax, you are not charged any basic-rate income tax on the profits that you might make from the bond. So, if you are a basic-rate taxpayer, there is no further tax for you personally to pay. But remember, even though you have not had to pay any tax, the insurance company has paid it for you, so your investment has not been tax free.

Sometimes these onshore investment bond bags are suggested because you are allowed to draw out part of your original investment each year without an immediate income tax charge. Be careful how this is presented to you. The tax rules let you take out up to 5% of your original investment each year in this way but this does not mean the investments inside the bag are necessarily earning 5%. That depends on what the recipe of investments is doing, it might be less or it might be more. These withdrawals are added up later and added to the value of the bag when you want it to come to an end or you want to take a larger chunk out. This is to see if there is any income tax for you to pay then. This can be especially useful if you are a higher-rate taxpayer now, but in the future, expect to be paying tax at a lower rate when you decide to cash in the bond, for example, because you will have retired.

If you are a higher rate taxpayer and likely to stay that way then when you cash in your bond, if you have made profits you will have to pay some tax.

Be careful if an onshore investment bond is the only option discussed with you, as they are not as attractive for many people as some of the other options available, but they are very popular with some advisers and some banks. I have spoken to a couple of advisers who used to work for banks who told me they were always under significant pressure to meet sales targets and that their bonuses, indeed their actual jobs, depended on meeting them. Often when I analyse a new clients existing investments, I am shocked at the level of commission that some investment bonds have paid to the adviser. Moreover, there was the client thinking that the advice was coming free!

OFFSHORE INVESTMENT BONDS

Don't be put off knowing about these because they are *offshore*, they are often set up in places like the Isle of Man, the Channel Islands, Gibraltar or Dublin and they are not, as many people think, tax avoidance schemes, or only for the very wealthy. Some of these offshore jurisdictions have similar investor protection to the UK, but it is always wise to make sure that this is checked, as it is an important point.

Because they are not based here in the UK, the insurance companies who provide these investments do not have to pay tax if the investments inside the bag make profit. Instead tax is paid when you decide to actually take the money out. This is sometimes called *gross rollup*, in other words any profits being made inside the bag are growing virtually tax free whilst the money sits inside. There is sometimes a small amount of tax that the insurance company has to pay on certain types of income that the bag might receive called withholding tax, which they can't claim back.

In the same way as an onshore bond can give you 5% of your original investment out of the bag each year without worrying about tax at the time, so can an offshore bond.

The biggest difference between the two types of bonds is that you can have some control over the tax that might need to be paid with an offshore bond. You can organise the offshore version to minimise the amount of tax you might have to pay by deciding when to take more than the 5% out. For example, if you are a higher rate taxpayer at the moment but you know that you are likely to drop down to being a lower rate tax payer in the future, waiting until you move down the tax bands could be a good time to take money out. At that point, your "profit" will be calculated and divided by how many years you have had your bond. This is added into the taxman's measuring jug and, depending on where on the scale the money from the bag sits, that's the rate or rates of tax you will pay, so it could be 0%, 20%, 40% or 45% or a mixture of two rates.

Another way offshore bonds can be used cleverly is if you wanted to give someone else money. Say your granddaughter is now at university and you would like to help fund her fees. Most offshore bonds are segmented, in other words they are a bit like an orange. You could "assign" a segment to your granddaughter, who could then cash in the investment to use it and this would be taxed in her hands not yours. So, if she has no other income, any profits the investment has made, if they fall within the first slice of her jug, will be tax free. Just be sure you discuss this with your financial planner or your solicitor, as you will need to keep an eye on the Inheritance Tax position to make sure you don't trip up on another tax.

It certainly is worth making sure you arrange your affairs in the best way to maximise what you have and to be able to make the most of your money for your family too.

PENSIONS

123

Put the Government State Pension to one side and think about a pension bag that you can *choose* to invest into, such as a private pension or your employer's pension scheme. This pension bag has a unique tax advantage compared with the other bags. If you are a basic rate tax payer, for every £80 you put into your pension bag, the tax man adds another £20. In other words, you would have had to earn £100 in the first place to be left with £80 after the tax man has taken his 20% income tax. He then gives you back the £20 you have already paid in tax (as a tax refund) by adding it to your pension for you, your pension company will make sure they claim it on your behalf. This means a total of £100 is invested into the bag but you have only put in £80 yourself. The reason behind this is the government wants us all to save for our old age so encourage us by giving a tax refund boost to our pension bags.

Oddly, even if you are a non-tax payer, you can still pay into a pension and the taxman will add the same amount to your bag as the basic rate taxpayer within certain limits.

If you are a higher rate taxpayer paying 40% tax on some of your income, when you invest £80 into your pension bag the taxman will put in £20 in the same way. But, because you have actually paid another £20 in tax to him you can claim this back from him too. Either you will get a refund, or a reduced tax bill or your income tax code will be altered to make sure you pay less tax. What this means is that if you are a higher rate taxpayer, once you have told him about your pension payment on your tax return it will only cost you £60 to have £100 invested in your pension bag, as the taxman gives you £20 back and adds £20 into the pension bag.

It would cost a 45% tax payer £55 to have a pension payment of £100 going into their pension.

There are limits to the amount you can invest into a pension and claim tax relief. This is the name for the amount the taxman puts into your bag. It is important to make sure you know how this works in your own case, if you decide to look at building up a pension for yourself.

The pension bag itself only pays a small amount of tax on the investments it holds. When you reach the point in time when you want to begin to take your pension (the earliest is age 55) the rules allow you to take out a quarter of the bag as a tax free lump sum. The rest of the bag is then used to create some income for you. Usually the way this is done is to use the pension bag to buy an **annuity**. An annuity is a swap of your pension bag for a smaller "purse" each month, normally for the rest of your life. Sometimes described as *buying an annuity*, your pension bag buys you your income.

This annuity income will be poured into the tax measuring jug to see how much tax you will be paying, as it is treated like a salary.

When you reach that point of wanting to take your pension as income, you must think of this as another crossroads in your financial planning. Stop and consider. Don't just accept the annuity, in other words the income purse your pension bag provider offers you. You might find that, if you shop around, you can move your bag to another pension company and they might pay you more income. This is known as an **open market option** and can make a real difference to the amount you might get. The best plan here is to take some advice so that, when you make the decision, you know you have really checked what is available and what type of annuity is best for you. There are a few choices to make to ensure you choose the right one for you and there are also some bows and whistles that might be worth adding.

This open market option is an important point to remember if your husband has a pension that gives you the option of buying an annuity in your own name. Your husband may have had a pension bag where, instead of swapping the pension bag to buy an annuity, he may have been taking money out of the bag whilst it still stayed in place. This is known as **drawdown**. If you have inherited your husband's drawdown bag, you will probably have several options that you will need to choose from, including in most cases, buying an annuity. If you are in this position, it is really important for you to take advice from a good and trusted financial planner that you feel comfortable with as, once you have made a decision on an annuity, you normally can't change your mind, so it needs to be right first time.

Your store of investments

I have already said at the start of the book I have not covered all of the detail you will need to be able to choose which, if any, of the above investment bags could be right for you. I would simply like you to have a better mental picture of these different bags so that, if they are suggested, or you already have some, you will at least have some basic information to work with and the questions that you will need to ask might come more easily. There is no substitute for an experienced, trustworthy adviser, and you might be better armed to spot someone who isn't considering all the options if you have a bit of knowledge. Having shown you what bags you might have, let's look at your cupboard again with some of these on the shelves.

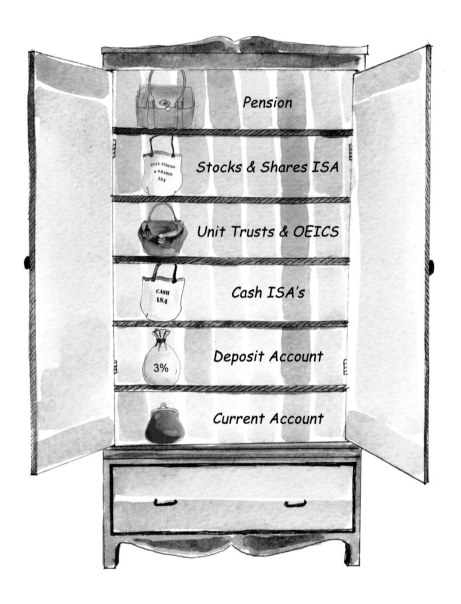

Pension

Stocks & Shares ISA

Unit Trusts & OEICS

Cash ISA's

Deposit Account

Current Account

10

How to Choose the Right Trusted Adviser

"Nobody can go back and start a new beginning, but
anyone can start today and make a new ending"

Anonymous

*H*aving someone who is experienced as a financial guide may be the single most important step you can take to make your progress to becoming financially well organised, a quicker and smoother process. Choosing the right person to help you is vital and well worth taking some time over. Some widows "inherit" their husband's financial adviser not really considering that this may not be the best or most helpful route. In this situation, it will be useful to read this chapter to help you really think about whether that person fits the bill for you.

Your needs in a relationship with an adviser may be different from your husband's and you must remember that you must put yourself first, not other people's feelings.

Most widows realise that they would probably do better with help but they are not sure where to turn.

An important title to look for is someone who is an independent financial adviser (IFA). Some, including myself, are known as financial planners. This is different from an adviser who is linked to a particular bank or insurance company, as only an independent adviser/planner can give you advice across all financial products available in the whole of the market. Many people are surprised to learn that even the private banks who serve the wealthy tend to sell their own products, which is not ideal if it's not the right thing.

To find truly unbiased and impartial advice use an independent financial planner who charges fees. The adviser will be paid by you, putting your interests first, working with you to make sure they understand your situation, providing you with comprehensive financial planning.

I have seen so many widows who have been sold products because that was the only way the adviser could be paid or they had targets to meet to justify their salary.

Often this leads to widows not actually getting what they need, which might be help organising their affairs better, being shown how what they already have works, real support and advice and not just sales patter. By paying for the advice you can avoid the type of conflicts of interest that I have seen where the right advice is not to take out the latest "whizz bang" investment; the best advice may be, for example, to reduce debt instead.

The good news is that there are significant changes in 2013 affecting the financial services world. These will create a more transparent environment for the consumer with some new legislation called the Retail Distribution Review. For those of us who have always agreed with our clients how we are paid, this will not be a big change, but there will be advisers who will not be able to adapt to this shift from being paid commission by the product providers. There will be some who will also struggle to meet the increased qualification requirements and so I believe that there will be fewer advisers in the future to serve the public, but hopefully some of the more unscrupulous will be amongst those that will not survive.

Often, as I do with my clients, a good financial planner will be able to create a model of your financial position by using a computer program to show you a visual picture of your finances so you can look at some "what if?" scenarios. This will be useful for you to see how far your tank will take you into the future, looking to see if it is likely to run out of money too soon and if so what you might be able to do to stop that happening. They will be able to show you how to protect and make the most of your resources.

If your position looks very secure a good financial planner will be able to help you work out how to reduce any Inheritance Tax (IHT) that your children may have to pay on your death. See Chapter 11 for more on IHT.

A special relationship

The relationship you will have with your financial planner is much more than just focussing on money. Of course, it is about budgeting, investing, tax planning and estate planning, which might sound very boring. However, it should be interesting because all of these things should be related to your life, your values, things that matter most to you.

For many financial planners, their relationships with their clients will last for years. My first widow client and I still work together meeting, each year for the past 22 years. Together we have navigated through some stormy waters, not always choppy because of money, but because sometimes family life can be "interesting". I know her well and she trusts me to give her clarity and the confidence to make decisions. As her decision partner I can help her but ultimately she makes the decisions herself, but doesn't feel she has had to make them on her own.

By having a good relationship with a trusted adviser who understands your financial position you might also avoid falling into the trap of feeling that you can't actually spend your money on yourself if everything looks stable.

One of my clients, Margaret has a really good level of income and much more capital than she will ever need during her lifetime. She was born before 1945 and so finds it difficult to spend money without a significant purpose. At one of our meetings we discussed what holidays she might want to take and she really struggled to think about what she wanted to do. I knew that she had a great relationship with both her children, their partners and her grand children and so I suggested that she could create an annual holiday that she could pay for.

We discussed different options and plumped for a large house in France with a swimming pool for a week. She would pay for the house and the two car ferry crossings and in exchange, everyone was to wait on her hand and foot!

She loved the idea but thought it would be too costly and might reduce the money in her tank too much. I was able to show her the effect of paying for this for a year and there was hardly any change to her numbers, and so we plugged this event in for five years which did alter the picture but not by much as she was in the very fortunate position of having plenty flowing into an already very buoyant tank. She was absolutely delighted and both families were thrilled. And as you can imagine these holidays became the highlight of her year.

Without the ability to see the financial picture and create a "what if" together with someone like myself and, strange as this sounds, giving her permission to spend, Margaret would not have had the confidence to "buy experiences and invest in memories".

It's a gift that will last forever and not something that she would have expected a financial planner to suggest.

Having the right adviser who will relate well to you and understand both your worries and what is important to you is so vital. They must *get you*, be able to communicate clearly and comfortably with you and ideally be used to helping widows with the problems they face.

A good place to start to find the right adviser for you is to ask your solicitor if he or she can recommend a suitable independent adviser. Another good source is the website for the Institute of Financial Planning, a not for profit organisation focused on raising awareness of the importance of good financial planning. Members include some of the most highly qualified and knowledgeable planners in the UK and the site has a search facility to find one in your area. The address is www.financialplanning.org.uk and the site is also a good source of general information on financial planning.

After making a shortlist of perhaps two or three, arrange a meeting with each of them. Most advisers will offer an initial meeting with no costs so that each of you can find out about the other. This might sound like hard work but it is vital that you find someone you can talk to easily, who listens to you and has good communication skills to be able to explain important financial topics in a way that is easy to understand.

One point I make to my clients is that if they are struggling to understand something it is me who is at fault as I am not explaining it well enough. That might be a useful thing to remember if you are ever in that situation. Perhaps ask if something you are struggling with can be explained again in a different way.

Back to the meetings, don't be surprised if you feel a bit nervous about going to this type of meeting; many people do until they have developed a good relationship.

Don't assume you will be asked lots of questions you won't understand or be unable to answer, it should be a supportive reassuring experience. Once again, if you are feeling unsure you could ask a family member or your trusted friend to go with you to that first meeting, and remember your note book so that you or your companion can write information down at each meeting. You will then be able to compare notes of the meetings afterwards. I would write the questions below in your notebook before each meeting. That way you will have some useful direct comparisons.

Useful questions to ask

When you meet a financial planner for the first time, you may like to ask questions like these:

- *Do you have any particular area of expertise?*

- *What type of clients do you normally work with?*

  In your situation, you don't really want an adviser whose main area of work is corporate pensions for limited companies! Listen for the type of work that you think would be useful for you.

- *Can you talk me through the process that you go through with a new client and how many meetings you expect us to have?*

This will tell you, first that they do have a process, which is better than not having one and then whether it sounds logical. Does it sound like it would help you? I have included a description below of my process, which will give you an idea of what you should be looking for. This process will take at least three meetings, often more.

My process looks like this:

Step 1 Foundation – Gather together the information needed, start to create your own system and begin to pick up the pieces

Step 2 Focus – What do you have? How can you make the most of it? What does your "Money Flow" look like?

Step 3 Future – How far will it take you? Will you have to make changes? Are you building wealth or running out?

Step 4 Financially organised – Settle and take stock

Step 5 Flying solo – Each year meet to check you are on track. What's changed? Where would you like to be? What do you want to do? For yourself? For your children? For others?

Back to questions for your prospective adviser

- *Will you be the only person working with me?*

  Ideally, if someone else will be working with you it is useful for you to meet them.

- *What services do you offer? Is it comprehensive financial planning or advice just on specific areas?*

- *How will I pay for your work with me?*

  Typically, planners are paid in a few different ways:

  Fees can be on an hourly rate like a solicitor or fees can be an agreed amount for a particular piece of work.

  A fee can be charged to establish an investment portfolio, often a set percentage of the amount to be invested. Then, typically, a set percentage or minimum amount is charged each year to look after the investments and provide on-going financial planning.

- *Can I speak to one of your clients who has been widowed so I can have a personal testimonial?*

  This should not cause a good planner a problem at all. From a practical point of view, I would explain in that situation that I would just make sure that my client was expecting you to call out of courtesy.

  You may feel it might be a bit odd to telephone a stranger to ask about the service and support they receive from their adviser but put yourself in that widow's shoes. Knowing what bereavement feels like, she may be only too glad to pass on a recommendation of a good financial planner, someone who has given her the right kind of help and support. She may be delighted to know she has helped you and her adviser by helping cement the relationship.

At that first meeting, the adviser will want to know something about you so that they can also establish that they are the right adviser for you. Listen carefully to the questions they ask, they should be interested in you and what's really important to you not just about your money.

By the time you have had your meetings with your shortlist, contacted some clients and reflected on your notes you may have enough information and will have probably decided who would be the best person to work with and with whom you are most likely to build up some trust. If you have inherited your husband's adviser why not ask him the same questions?

11

Putting your House in Order

"I can't change the direction of the wind, but I can adjust my sails to always reach my destination"

James Dean

*W*hen you are ready, one of the aspects of your finances you may want to review is your estate planning.

Making a will

Making sure you have a will that reflects your wishes is important, as dying without a valid will, known as dying "intestate" can create difficulties for those left behind trying to cope with not only a bereavement but more red tape. Making sure you leave a will means that you can decide how your possessions and money will be distributed – if you don't, the law says who gets what and it may not be what you would want.

It is never easy making a will as no one really wants to confront the thought of their end of life planning, and so it tends to be one of those things that is important but not urgent, and often complicated, so other easier jobs are done instead. It might become urgent but it could be too late to do anything about it. You may already have a will in place, perhaps you and your husband arranged your wills at the same time. There is no such thing as a joint will and often when husbands and wives make their wills together, these two separate documents are sometimes known as "Mirror Wills" which will usually be more or less identical hence the reason they are called mirror wills.

It is a good idea to think about whether your will does do what it needs to do now that your life has changed. For example are your executors, the person or people you have chosen to deal with the practical administration of your estate and carry out your instructions, still the most suitable?

Are your children grown up and quite capable of carrying out this task? I have met clients who have been persuaded to appoint their bank as an executor and I would urge you to think carefully about this if you have already done so or it has been suggested.

One client's mother had appointed the bank as an executor together with her son and on her death had a very simple estate, a few deposit accounts and a house. The son, my client, did all the work to sort out the estate, having to arrange for the bank to sign various documents and at the end of the process the bank charged over £13,000 as this was written into the paperwork that his mother had signed. We tried making a formal complaint but got nowhere. Neither he nor I knew that this was the way that her will had been written because as often happens in families, he had not wanted to talk to her about a subject that he felt could make him sound grasping or greedy. It is probably best if you bring up the subject with your family and try to be open and matter of fact with them. It is not an easy subject for anyone to talk about but it is better to discuss things together if possible. If there is any possibility of family arguments or possible mistrust between any members of the family, think about appointing a solicitor as an executor who can act as an independent person in the process.

An example of a widow taking control of her own financial affairs was my client Stephanie. Stephanie was Philip's second wife; his first died when his two children were very young and during their marriage together they were never able to have children of their own.

Stephanie worked all her life as a teacher and then head teacher but Philip was the one who organised all the finances for the two of them during their marriage. Many years before he died, Philip organised wills for Stephanie and himself, which left half of the value of their home in a trust for his two children, giving Stephanie the right to live in the house for the rest of her lifetime. Everything else was left to Stephanie. Her will then said that on her death everything she had went to Philip's two children.

Around four years after Philip's death Stephanie and I discussed her will, which she had never really thought about before. Looking at what would happen on her death she felt that, as some of the assets that she owned were from her own working life, and from her own mother's estate, she wanted to make some changes. The bulk of her assets would still go to her two step-children but she changed her will so that she made some gifts of money and personal items to her nieces and nephews and some gifts were made to some local charities that were very close to her heart. She felt really content after her new will had been organised, saying she thought it felt right that she had now put her own wishes into place, knowing that everything felt more balanced. It may be that your will needs no changes but as part of your steps to taking control of your finances you should relook at it.

Appointing Trustees

If your children are under 18 and you were to die leaving them with no living parent and no will, the Court would decide who would take on the role of guardians. Neither you nor your family will have any control over this. That is one reason why making a will is crucial as you can choose who you would want to look after your children. Before appointing any guardians, it is sensible to discuss this with whomever you choose to make sure that they are willing to take on that role and for you to talk through some of the practical aspects that would be important to you. There is another role that would be of vital importance in this situation and that is the role of your Trustees. The assets that you leave to your children would be protected inside a **trust** as they would be too young to take control of the money and property themselves. As part of your estate planning you will need to appoint Trustees to "caretake" these assets for your children.

As the name suggests, Trustees must be people you trust. They can be the same people as your guardians but that might not be the best solution. Say, for example, you have a sister who would be the ideal guardian for your children but finds money matters difficult, but your brother is really good with paperwork and money, you could appoint your sister as guardian and your sister and brother as Trustees together.

A letter of wishes

A **letter of wishes** that sits alongside your will can be a very useful and positive document. Your husband may have written a letter of wishes himself. If you found that it helped you to know some of his feelings, it would perhaps be comforting for your family to have your wishes recorded. Unlike a will this is not a legal document and so will not become public, you can write it yourself and it does not need to be witnessed. A letter of wishes cannot be binding on your executors and trustees, in other words, it is guidance to help them make some choices, however you cannot order them to take your guidance. Think of it as a very personal letter or letters in which you can give instructions and guidance on virtually any subject related to your affairs.

For example, if you have young children you may say in your letter that you would be happy for the Trustees to use some of the money for education purposes or that if your child needed medical help money could be used for that purpose.

On a different note, you might want to help your executors plan your burial or cremation and tell them that you would prefer people not to spend money on flowers; that you would like a particular charity to receive a donation instead or that you would like the music to be a particular song or piece. It makes it far easier for your family if you are able to help them with these difficult decisions.

If you want to leave specific items to people, include a clause in your will so that "personal chattels will be distributed in accordance with any letter of wishes". Use your letter of wishes to give a detailed description if you know that someone close to you may like a particular personal possession. This will make it easier for items to be correctly identified and passed on. Make sure you say who will receive the rest of your personal possessions in your letter. It can be useful to have the flexibility to deal with your personal items such as jewellery in a letter that you can change easily rather than having to alter your will.

If you have chosen to leave someone out of your will, your letter of wishes could add some weight so that if there was a challenge, your executors would have more evidence of your wishes. It may be wise if you are leaving someone out of your will who might try to make a challenge, to talk this through with a solicitor as there are cases where wills have been overturned by disgruntled relatives. It's best to make sure your wishes are in place robustly in this type of scenario.

A letter of wishes can be easily updated, just make sure that you date it correctly and destroy any old ones so that there is no confusion. Keep it sealed and labelled with your important documents, such as your own copy of your will.

The following is an example of the way a typical letter of wishes would be laid out:

Private & Confidential
Letter of wishes to My Executors, and Trustees, My Family and My Beneficiaries and Any Other Person Whom It May Concern:

I, (name), of (address), wish to state my wishes with respect to certain items of sentimental value, my personal chattels, my gifts to charity and my funeral wishes:

This Letter of Wishes does not change or revoke my Will.

I request that the following items be given to the individuals or charities indicated below:

Description of Item   Name of Person/Charity to Receive

The rest of my chattels I leave to

```
┌─────────────────────────────────────────────────────────────────┐
│  My Funeral wishes are:                                           │
│                                                                   │
│                                                                   │
│                                                                   │
│  Signature and date                                               │
│                                                                   │
└─────────────────────────────────────────────────────────────────┘
```

If when your husband died the funeral arrangements had been pre-planned, you will know what a relief it was to know you were following his wishes. It will be just as important to make sure your own wishes are clear and known, so including them in your letter of wishes will make a difficult time easier for those you love. Think about writing another letter to those who are most precious to you telling them how you feel about them. I am sure that finding such a letter with your papers would be a real comfort.

Inheritance Tax

When thinking about your estate planning it is useful to have some knowledge of Inheritance Tax (IHT)

Inheritance tax needs to be paid only in certain circumstances. Husbands and wives and civil partners are treated differently to everyone else in that when possessions move on death between these couples there is no IHT to pay.

It is when the last person in these partnerships dies and passes their assets to, say, their children or grandchildren that the situation changes. We can leave a certain amount tax free to anyone on our death and this amount has a special name, the Nil Rate Band. Back to measuring jugs and the tax man. The band that is liable for tax at nil rate (in other words 0% rate of tax) for the tax year April 2013 to April 2014 is £325,000. Here is an example:

Tom dies leaving everything he has to his wife Barbara. When Barbara dies her estate including the house and everything else she owns is worth £550,000, which she leaves to her children. Because Tom didn't use any of his nil rate tax band (£325,000) their children can use this up on top of

Barbara's £325,000 if they apply to use it. Remember though, it is not automatic. They will need a copy of Tom's will, a copy of their parents' marriage certificate and a copy of the grant of probate issued on his death, as well as any deeds of variation that might have been done at the time of Tom's death. It is worth letting your children know where these documents are and this shows how important it is to keep your paperwork orderly.

ESTATE FLOW FOR TOM AND BARBARA

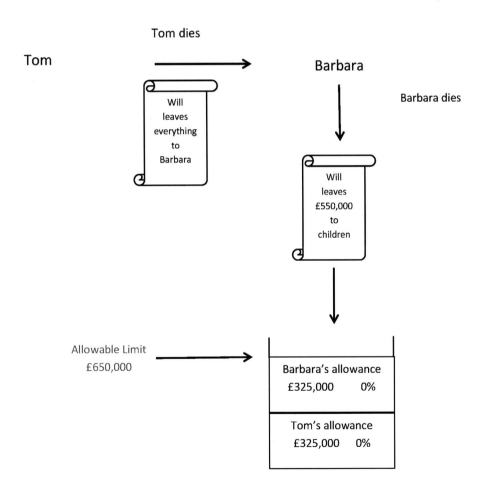

As the value of Barbara's estate (£550,000) is less than the two nil rate bands added up together (£325,000 + £325,000) there will be no Inheritance tax to pay.

Let's look at a larger estate:

Jerry dies leaving everything to Margot. When Margot dies her estate including the house and everything else she owns is worth £750,000, which she leaves to her children.

As Jerry didn't use any of his nil rate band on his death, he gave everything to Margot, their children can also soak up his allowance on top of Margot's following the same process as Tom and Barbara. However, the value of the estate will be bigger than both of their allowances added together and so some tax has to be paid.

ESTATE FLOW FOR JERRY AND MARGOT

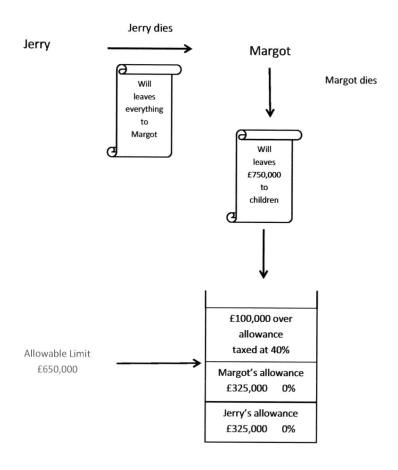

At the moment (2013) the Inheritance Tax rate is 40%. This means Jerry and Margot's children will face a bill of 40% of £100,000. Which means £40,000 will have to be paid to the tax man.

Because house prices have gone up so much in the last few years, more people have found themselves in the group whose children will have to pay inheritance tax.

There are ways to reduce the amount of tax that your children may have to pay by planning during your lifetime but you should take expert advice, as that way you will make sure that you use the best route for you, making sure that your own position is secure first.

Lasting Powers of Attorney

So far, we have looked at making sure that when you die your wishes are carried out. Another important part to putting your house in order is to think about making a **Lasting Power of Attorney** (LPA) if you haven't already done so. This is a legal document giving someone else, your attorney or attorneys, the ability to make certain decisions on your behalf. There are two different types of LPA; the first one covers your property and financial affairs if you, for example, go into hospital or lose the mental capacity to deal with your own arrangements and need someone to do that for you, the second type deals with your health and welfare, but this one only comes into action if you become unable to make those decisions for yourself.

A point to bear in mind here is that if you are in Scotland or Northern Ireland there may be different terminology and rules compared with those in England.

Because of the role that this person takes on you must think carefully about who would be suitable. You can appoint more than one person and you can decide how they would work together. For example, you might have three children and appoint them all. You would decide if they could act independently, in other words, could one of them deal with paying your bills or do all three have to act together and all sign cheques, for example. Legally, your attorney must be over 18 and not be bankrupt if they are going to step into your shoes to look after your financial affairs and, of course, you must trust them to act in your best interests.

These LPA's replaced the older style Enduring Power of Attorney (EPA) in October 2007, which can still be used if you have one to look after your financial affairs but they do not cover your health and welfare.

A word of caution here; once you lack the ability to deal with your own affairs and you need your attorneys to take over, the Power of Attorney has to be **registered**, in other words "activated". Thereafter your attorneys must act in *your* best interests, and cannot make any "financial gifts" (for example to themselves) other than small gifts for birthdays etc. A friend of mine who had given up her career to look after her mother fell foul of the rules on powers of attorney. She was her mother's attorney and even though her mother wanted to help her financially, once her mother went into a nursing home and the Power of Attorney had to be registered, her mother no longer had the power help her – the Power of Attorney forbids attorneys from "making gifts to themselves". My friend had no means of supporting herself and was put into a financial crisis. So, although the Power of Attorney was the right thing to have organised, in their situation they needed to understand its limitations and plan accordingly.

Don't however, let the above tale put you off considering taking this organisational step. If you don't have any powers of attorney in place and you become unable to look after your own affairs an application would have to be made to the Court of Protection, who would choose and appoint "a deputy" who would have to report to the court, keeping accounts and putting up a security bond. The court may not choose the same person you would and the court appointed route is both time consuming and costly.

Like making a will, this is an important but normally not urgent thing to organise, however, unfortunately if you begin to lose capacity you may also have already lost the chance to put yourself in control by choosing who might look after your affairs. This step is also vital if there is any possibility of family arguments or mistrust. This is often difficult to contemplate, however you must be very realistic when you consider this, don't just think of how you would expect people to behave, think about how they are likely to do things if you were unable to look after your own affairs. When relooking at your will ask your solicitor to talk to you about organising a LPA if you don't already have one.

When you feel you can make a start on this part of your financial affairs, use the list of questions below to gather together some of the information you will need and record it here as you go in preparation.

Do you have a will in place?

If so, where is the original?

Who are your executors?

Are they the right people? Did you make your will many years ago when your children were under age? Would it make sense to appoint them now?

Do you have children who are under eighteen? Who have you appointed in your will as guardians?

Who would be the best people to act as your Trustees? Ideally, you should choose at least two to act together.

It can sometimes be sensible to appoint different people to have the responsibility of dealing with the financial and administrative aspects of your estate from the people who have the practical responsibility of caring for your children.

Who is financially dependent on you, if anyone?

Who do you want to benefit from the assets that you own?

List them down.

Do you want them to have an equal share or different amounts?

Are you leaving anyone out who may try to make a claim after you die?

Do you want to leave anything to a particular charity?

Do you have an old Enduring Power of Attorney in place? Remember in Scotland and Northern Ireland it will be known as a different name but will probably include the term "Power of Attorney".

Do you know if it came to an end when you lost your husband?

Who would be the best person or people to appoint to look after your affairs if you were not able to do so yourself?

These are just a few thoughts that you need to gather before you make a start on actually changing an old will or creating a new one, or putting into place a Lasting Power of Attorney.

If you don't already have a suitable solicitor, consider finding one who is a member of The Society of Trust and Estate Practioners (STEP). These solicitors are considered to be the most experienced in the field of estate planning. A search can be done on www.step.org

Doing all of this is a great gift for those you love and shows just how much you care.

12

Looking Ahead to the Future

"When one door of happiness closes, another opens, but often we look so
long at the closed door that we do not see the one that has
been opened up for us"

Helen Keller

*T*here is no doubt in my experience that when you have, little by little, taken charge of your own financial affairs you will feel more grounded. You will feel better about your future. You will still be feeling the pain of your loss and you cannot underestimate the time it takes to come to terms with a different life. However, by feeling that your feet are on the ground, knowing how your financial position looks will provide you with some much-needed stability to be able to take steps forward.

This applies even if your financial position is weak as, by knowing how the land lies, you will be able to make decisions rather than living in anxiety and fear about an unknown set of circumstances. It is even more important if you are in this position to find out exactly how things are and how they will look going forward so that you can make sure you are making choices rather than burying your head and finding that events overtake you.

Without exception, widows I have worked with have, given time and the right information and support, become financially well organised. Some widows have surprised themselves at how capable they actually are in what they perceived as the minefield of money. Indeed women have many of the qualities that are needed to have good financial plans and investments in place.

One of these qualities, unlike some men, is that women are not overconfident about their own knowledge and opinions, meaning that they will take advice and tend not to become investment greedy, which can lead to unnecessary risk-taking. I think also that women find it easier to accept the idea that simplicity is the ultimate form of sophistication. Simple solutions are sometimes resisted because people expect something very complicated. Remember it sometimes suits people to bamboozle you with complicated stuff but it really doesn't need to be like that.

If you can deal with each part of your life and finances in a straightforward manner then I think that's the way to go. Remember, we were born with the ability to multitask and this also applies to our financial affairs, once we get one plate spinning well, we can move on and get another up and going.

Finding your feet and stepping forwards

So thinking about the future, what can you do to bring some light into what seems to be all darkness?

A client of mine, Jean told me of the turning point in her life. She said she came to realise that she had to decide whether to deal with the grief and then prepare to get on with a different life or to continue to make her suffering itself a new way of life. She decided to move ahead positively, wanting to create a new life. Although it was so very hard at times, she has done what she decided to do and is now more fulfilled and positive about the future than she ever thought she could be.

The fact is there is no going back; you have to look to the future.

Be aware though that women can be their own worst enemies. Imagine a friend who constantly criticises you, the way you look, your shape, your abilities, the things you do, the things you don't do. You wouldn't want to be around that friend and may decide that someone who can't see the good in you is not worth spending time with. That friend is the little voice in your head, the monkey on your shoulder constantly chattering to you about all things negative, whispering seductively, never being quiet.

Here's the good news, you can control that monkey voice. You can choose to ignore it or think about a little angel on the other shoulder responding with positives. You need to make your angel stronger than the monkey so that when he tells you "you can't" your angel tells you she knows you can. Listen to her, make her voice stronger and your monkey voice will lose power. Your angel sees all the best things in you because she knows they are there. How would your angel describe the best things about you?

A client Beryl concluded she needed help to move forward and so she decided that when she felt insecure or anxious, she would ask herself what her friend Margaret would do. Margaret is very organised and outgoing and seems to take all things in her stride. Rather than allowing herself to be intimidated by Margaret's strengths, Beryl used her as a role model and this helped her to start to form new habits which over time became easier to follow. Beryl's path became steadier to walk as she looked for a way to support herself.

Acting as the person you want to be can be really useful and in time will feel more natural, enabling you to conquer some of the problems that you might have thought were insurmountable.

Helen had a different problem, she had a really difficult time when she occasionally felt okay and even began to laugh at things again. Her problem was that she felt guilty if she laughed or enjoyed anything after her husband died. Here is something to think about in that situation, perhaps a note on the fridge might help:

"Prescription for Laughter
One dose twice a day.

Increase the size and frequency of dose
until it becomes easier to swallow."

Don't be afraid like Helen was. As well as recognising the need for grieving you must also not be afraid to live and don't be afraid to look forward.

Try this

Don't think too far ahead at the moment, just take some time to visualise and imagine you are sitting here three years from today.

If we were here looking back over those three years what would have needed to happen for you to feel happy with your progress?

> What was in the way for you to bump into?
>
> What strengths and support did you have to help you?

Feeling wealthy

There may be times when it is hard to see anything other than an uncertain future, economic crises, inflation, bad news stories from around the world, together with all the grief and other emotions that come as part and parcel of bereavement. When you step back and consider that there is an abundance and richness in your life with experiences that will bring joy such as family, friends, home, health, faith, purpose and more, you are indeed wealthy. Sometimes we forget it is all there.

Two psychologists studied the impact of asking people to write about gratitude. Three groups were asked to spend a few moments each week writing. One group was asked to write about the things they were grateful for, another group was asked to write about things that annoyed them and the final group was required to write about events that had happened that week.

The gratitude group ended up happier, healthier, more optimistic and even exercised more than the other two groups.

Everyone has something to be happy about, often we just stop noticing what it is. In your particular situation, it is even more important for you to bring to mind those thoughts. It might be a good idea at this point to try to keep your position in perspective by thinking about where you fit in the world's population.

You are probably wealthier than you think.

> *If you woke up this morning with more health than illness, you are more blessed than one million who will not survive this week.*
>
> *If you have never experienced the danger of battle, the loneliness of imprisonment, the agony of torture or the pangs of starvation, you are ahead of 500 million people on the planet.*
>
> *If you can attend a church, synagogue or other place of worship without fear of harassment, arrest, torture or death you are more blessed than three billion people in the world.*
>
> *If you have food in the fridge, clothes on your back, a roof over your head and a place to sleep you are richer than 75% of the people on the planet.*
>
> *If you have money in the bank and in your purse you are amongst the 8% most wealthy people in the world.*

"There are people who have money and people who are rich"
Coco Chanel

When we step back and see the positive things in our lives perhaps compared to others, it can make us feel more grounded and less anxious or resentful of where we feel we are today. In time you may re-read this and recognise that you have indeed realised that you are wealthy in many ways.

Don't become obsessed with money, it is important but it is simply the tool with which you can sort out the stuff that really matters.

Keeping everything in perspective, what special wealth do you enjoy?

As you move beyond the difficulties you have to face and feel more in control of your life, you might feel the time is right for you to begin to think about what is important to you and what you want to do for yourself. This may be difficult, especially if you have always put other people's needs above your own, often the way that women, especially mothers are.

Try this

As time passes, you will find thinking about the future easier and your thoughts and ideas are likely to change. When you feel ready, look at the list below and add to it as you see things more clearly and begin to feel more in control of what is important for you.

WHO
Who do I want to spend time with?

Who do I want to get to know and develop friendships with?

WHERE
Where do I want to live?

Where do I want to spend time?

WHAT
What are the things that I want to do?

What do I want to learn?

What do I want for the rest of my life?

WHEN
When do I want to make a change if a change is needed?

WHY
Why do I feel the need for change?

Is this a good enough reason?

HOW

How can I make a change?

Physically?

Financially?

Socially?

Try this

Before you look at the picture below write today's date here

_____

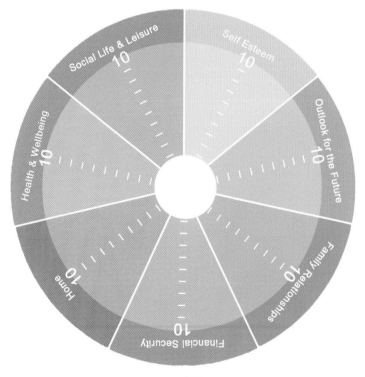

Be honest with yourself and put a dot on each subject line to record where you are at the moment, 10 being really positive, 0 being rock bottom.

After you have put a dot on each one, join them up around the circle.

When you look at the shape is it a circle or is it jagged with parts way out of balance?

Which is the one area that would bring a better shape quickest?

Do you feel you could focus on that segment?

What small step could you take to move your dot?

Put a note on your calendar to look at your circle in six months' time and add a note to the calendar to add a date to the following year's calendar again six months after that. When you do look at this again, see if any of your dots move, perhaps plot them in a different colour.

Hopefully you will have been able to move some of your dots towards the outer circle. If you find any have moved towards the middle see if you can focus on a small step to help you push it out again.

Building a new relationship with awareness

For some women, life after bereavement might be better than it was before, as not everyone is lucky enough to have a happy, loving marriage. Some women find that gaining a healthy measure of self-respect is life changing, having to go through the rigors of grief and surviving, having to make decisions can in themselves, be empowering. Others may find that the opportunity to change their lifestyles and use their skills and talents is satisfying and fulfilling. This doesn't mean that being married held you back, but being in a place where you can choose to go forward with a new beginning can in time be positively life changing.

At some stage, someone else might come into your life. You might not be able to contemplate this yet, but it may happen. You may even decide you want a more permanent relationship with them.

For some widows it is impossible to imagine any one measuring up to their late husband, but sometimes they choose to only remember their husband's positive attributes and forget the habits and characteristics that drove them mad. Other widows focus on the negative aspects that went with their marriage and are determined that another relationship would never be on the cards.

The reality is that even imperfect available men are thin on the ground and the perfect ones only exist in films. The same of course goes for us; the perfect woman doesn't exist either.

But, if you have moved forward, becoming more independent and secure in yourself by having to work through both grief and becoming independent, having another relationship from this position will be different. Having been married before should give you an insight into what works and what doesn't and you will in time be able to think about what you would really like from a new relationship.

However, living alone can be much more enjoyable and rewarding than living with the wrong man.

Men are like fine wine.

They all start out as grapes,

and it's a woman's job

to stomp on them

and keep them in the dark

until they mature

into something

you'd like

to have dinner with.

When starting a new relationship, take things slowly and be careful in relation to your own money and assets, as there are men out there on the look out for a wealthy widow. There are also men who are worried that they might also just be a meal ticket, so be sensitive to this too. These days going dutch (each of you picking up your own share of a restaurant bill) is totally acceptable.

If your relationship develops and you start to talk marriage or buying a property together, as far as the financial side of the two of you coming together, being open with each other at that stage is a must.

If you are thinking about buying a joint property, think about who is bringing what to the table and what happens if either of you die or decide to split up. Sometimes buying a joint property when either one of you or both of you have children can be more complicated.

The usual way to buy a property together is to buy it jointly. This means that if one of you were to die the other would then inherit the other's share automatically. This might not be what you want if either of you have children. One way to deal with this is buy the property as "Tenants in Common".

This means that each of you owns an actual share of the house and you can then leave your share in your will to your children. Often this is done by putting your share on your death into a "trust" so that your new partner can continue to live in the house but your share will ultimately go to your children. Make sure that you are both able to talk about the financial side of your relationship openly, as I have already mentioned, as it can be an area of conflict. Talk this through with a solicitor to make sure before you buy the property you have worked out the nitty gritty.

If you are considering marriage again, I would recommend that you discuss and arrange a pre-nuptial agreement to make sure that each of you protects your own family in case the marriage fails or one of you dies. Some think that pre-nuptial agreements are only for the wealthy. I don't believe this is true; although more essential for the wealthy, given the high legal fees and stress involved in a divorce, the frequency with which relationships end nowadays, as well as people's increasing financial sophistication and independence, a pre-nuptial agreement can benefit just about everyone.

Another misconception is that pre-nuptial agreements are only useful if your relationship breaks down. Without a pre-nuptial agreement, your spouse may be able to invalidate your carefully thought out estate plan, so again it could be useful for both of you if you each have children. Again, meet with a solicitor to discuss this together and they will then be able to help you put the right agreements in place.

Of course, pre-nuptial agreements can be seen as unromantic, but being able to sit down and discuss your future financial plans and expectations for the relationship openly will lead to a more solid foundation than simply expecting your love to take care of everything.

Epilogue

*I*know there are many other areas that I could have written about that would be very useful for a widow. But, rather than cover every aspect that might be relevant, what I set out to achieve with this book was to show you a few simple steps and share some information that will help you along the road to feeling you are planting your feet back on the ground. I do hope that I have managed that.

With hope and encouragement,

Anita

'Yesterday is history
Tomorrow is a mystery
Today is a gift
That's why it's called the present'

Eleanor Roosevelt

Resources

Practical help, support groups and useful contacts

At the time of writing these internet links and telephone numbers were correct, but of course these details can change over time. If the details are out of date, at least you will know that the organisation or group exists and you might be able to find their latest information from somewhere else.

- **Anita Gatehouse**

  www.awidowsguide.co.uk

  and at

  cre8 Wealth Management

  www.cre8wm.co.uk

  Telephone 01562 745730

- **Help to find a suitable Financial Planner** -

  The Institute of Financial Planning

  www.financialplanning.org.uk

  Telephone 0117 945 2470

- **Cruse – A national charity set up to offer free advice to bereaved people**

  www.crusebereavementcare.org.uk

  Telephone 0844 477 9400

- **National Association of Widows**

  www.nawidows.org.uk

  Telephone 0845 838 2261

- **Gingerbread – Help and support for single parents**

  www.gingerbread.org.uk

  Telephone 0808 802 0925

- **Way Foundation Young (WAY) – widowed men and women supporting each other**

  www.wayfoundation.org.uk

  Telephone 0300 012 4929

- **Way Up – a self-help group supporting the needs of widowed people over the age of 50.**

  www.way-up.co.uk

- **NP45 – A guide to government bereavement benefits**

  www.dwp.gov.uk/docs/np-45

- **Consumer Credit Counselling Service**

  www.cccs.co.uk

- **Shelley Whitehead – Bereavement Coaching**

  www.motivationsynergy.com

  Telephone 0208 346 2192

- **Kristie West – Grief Specialist**

  www.kristiewest.com

  Email kristie@kristiewest.com

- **Fi Ivin – Stylist, confidence and career coach for women over 40**

  www.womenonawobble.com

  Telephone 01753 884 997

- **Sharon Agates and Agape Cottage – counsellor and psychotherapist.**
  Stays in a luxury cottage specifically for women in need of TLC.

  www.agapecottage.co.uk

  Telephone 07734 472478

- **Saga**

  www.saga.co.uk

  Telephone 01303 771 111

- **Women's Institute**

  www.thewi.org.uk

  Telephone 0207 371 9300

- **Age UK**

  www.ageuk.org.uk

  Telephone 0800 169 6565

Acknowledgements

There are many people I would like to acknowledge who have been fundamental in making this book a reality. My lovely widowed clients were my starting point, recollecting their individual journeys into a different life. Thank you each one of you. You have enriched my life.

My wonderful long-suffering assistant Jacqui has been my support for many years and scarily, knows my thoughts before I do. Thanks, you are the best.

My children, Sophie and Toby have had to be encouraging and supportive when I've been juggling lots of balls in the air. Thank you, I'm so lucky to have such gorgeous, lovely children.

My reviewers were kind enough to take time to read my draft book and feedback. Thank you Dennis, Jeff, Alan, Judy E, Jo, Jean, Darren, Sarah, Megan and James, for your lovely comments and ideas which were really useful and appreciated.

My illustrators Graham and Sarah, thank you both, you embraced my project and really tried to get on paper the pictures I had in my head, sometimes a difficult place to be!

Judy Dendy has been invaluable in proofreading and laying out my book, challenging me to rewrite sections that she felt needed to be simplified. Thank you Judy, the book is far better with your non-judgemental suggestions and encouragement.

Last but not least, my amazing husband John, who always believes in me, my rock and my best friend. Thank you is an understatement.

About the Author

$\mathcal{B}$ased in Worcestershire, Anita Gatehouse is passionate about delivering great financial planning solutions via her own wealth management business in Kidderminster. For over 25 years she has helped address her clients' financial needs with a professional, caring, down-to-earth approach. Her focus is always on the end result – how to help clients use their financial resources to take control of their lives and look after the people and things they care about. Anita specialises in working with retired couples, divorcees and business directors but it is her work with widows that has inspired her to become an author.

She is a member of the Institute of Financial Planning and a founder member of the EBIS Group (Evidence based Investment Solutions) a think tank for smarter investment startegies.

She is married with two children, has two dogs and loves travelling, dancing, especially Argentine Tango and cooking, particularly anything she's grown in her garden.